Fragments of utopia:
collage reflections of heroic modernism

David Wild

Fragments of utopia
collage reflections of heroic modernism

Hyphen Press | London

author's text and collages
copyright © David Wild, 1998

published by
Hyphen Press, London, 1998
designed by
Peter Brawne
production assistance
Sally Goble
text output in
Berthold Akzidenz-Grotesk medium
made in the Netherlands:
lithography and printing by
Drukkerij Rosbeek, Nuth
binding by
Handboekbinderij M Geertsen, Nijmegen

ISBN 0 907259 10 3

Contents

Introduction

To work with leftover materials, with the garbage and throwaways of our daily and commonplace existence, is an integral aspect of the tradition of modern art, as if it were a magic reversal of the informal into things of quality through which the artist comes to terms with the world of objects. No wonder then that if the most heartfelt condition today is that of wishing to salvage values pertinent to architecture, the only means is to employ 'war surplus' materials, that is, to employ what has been discarded on the battlefield after the defeat of the modern movement. Thus, the new 'knights of purity' advance into the realm of the present debate waving as flags the fragments of a utopia which they themselves cannot see.

Manfredo Tafuri, 1974

All that is solid melts…

Salvage and fragments were appropriate words for me when the record of some thirty years of architectural tourism went up in smoke one lunch hour in April 1990. A broken screw that should have held the damper blade fast to the vertical control rod of the Pither 'studio' stove allowed the apparently dead and damped-down fire to blaze up, reaching a temperature sufficient to ignite material in the cupboard above, which was packed too close to the insulated flue. Stacked on the narrow shelves above were several thousand slides, in plastic boxes, and smaller books. Tafuri's *Architecture and utopia*, a present from Haig Beck when editor of *Architectural Design*, was now at the centre of a charred wall of molten plastic. Not without a certain macabre fascination, the visual effect of this painful episode, might be termed 'Schmerzbau', with apologies to the memory of Kurt Schwitters.

The intense heat also melted the copper rising main, spraying water below. So, while the top of the house filled with smoke, the ground floor flooded. The structure of the hand-built concrete house survived this test by fire and water (the fire itself was contained within the protected enclosure of the staircase), and the salvage operation was the starting point for the first collages. The lean years of the Thatcher era certainly allowed ample time for reflection. One eventual result of this accidental, catastrophic editing, was to let me to focus again on early enthusiasms, as precious images and material survived the small *Auto da fé* – including Canetti's book, a birthday gift in 1962, now suitably scorched.

The architectural tourism had begun in earnest with a short

excursion to Holland, led by Ken Frampton in the sixties salad days at Douglas Stephen and Partners. Not 'De 8 en Opbouw', but eight of us in the Architectural Association minibus. Duiker's work was a revelation, and coffee served with Thomas's TC100 stacking china in the Van Nelle factory capped a memorable introduction to the wealth of Dutch modernism. A more recent visit, finding Duiker's work refurbished and still in use – especially the less published technical school at Scheveningen – confirmed the earlier admiration for this master of the 'nieuwe bouwen', and compensated for the present sad state of Zonnestraal and the Cineac cinema.

It was Ken Frampton, again, who provided an introduction to Camilla Gray and Russian constructivism. Her pioneering study *The great experiment: Russian art 1863–1922*, first published in 1962, earned the opprobrium of the Soviet Ministry of Culture, and (until 1969) she was refused re-entry to the USSR to marry her Russian fiancé. The early, revolutionary experiments had already been written out of history. This was confirmed again in 1971 when the Soviet minister of culture, visiting the inspiring 'Art in Revolution' exhibition in London, insisted that the 'proun room' of El Lissitzky be sealed off. The exhibition was originally planned to open the new Hayward Gallery, on the old Festival of Britain site, in 1968 – that revolutionary year. But with the Soviet invasion of Czechoslovakia – another confirmation of the degeneration of the original ideals of 1917 – the exhibition was postponed. The debates of the 1920s and 1930s in Russia on the relationship between architecture and society now found themselves condemned to unresolved repetition – no longer a matter of life and death, perhaps – as the cruel dynamic of market capitalism and fashion replaced the utopian socialist ideals: not necessarily the survival of the fittest, but certainly of the privileged. Some of the most talented young British architects, whose models had made such an impact at the 'Art in Revolution' exhibition, chose to follow Andrei Burov's example, and shifted from purism to pastiche.

The 1951 Festival of Britain, swan song of the reforming post-war Labour

Frampton *et al* at Aldo van Eyck's orphanage in Amsterdam, 1963

government, contained echoes of Leonidov's constructivist projects of the 1920s. The Skylon, in particular, stood alongside the more substantive Festival Hall. With the indecently swift demolition by the incoming Conservative government of the Skylon and other Festival structures, capped in November 1954 by the abolition of building licences, the property boom was on, and socialist planning off. The developers of this inflationary wave of building adopted Mies van der Rohe's 'less is more'; but in a market version, without the philosophical refinement of details. In other words: less cost equals more profit. A similar utilitarianism was the guiding force behind most local authority housing. The stage was set for a general rejection of what was understood as modern architecture. Instead of transcending the limits of functionalism – as already evidenced in such projects as Le Corbusier's weekend house of 1935, with its poetic fusion of vernacular, classical and technological elements – refuge was sought in nostalgia. With the abandonment of an earlier government's Parker Morris report on minimum standards in the house, now seen as an impossible maximum, the less fortunate found themselves once again in tiny cottages: but with far less space around, and tied not to an employer but to a crippling mortgage. The modern movement's 'minimum living standard', subject of the 1929 CIAM meeting in Frankfurt and drawn up at a time of crisis, was now adopted by private house builders in a time of plenty (for some). With the coming of the slump that must follow boom, a new phrase would enter the British language: 'negative equity'.

The brutalist bunker of the Hayward Gallery was designed by a team from the London County Council that included two members of the Archigram group: Ron Herron and Warren Chalk. By the 1970s, the heroic projects of Soviet constructivism – in particular, the design for *Struggle and victory* by Popova and Vesnin (1921) – found their pale echo in the consumerist fantasies of Archigram. And now mini-airships hover over suburban superstores. 'Hegel remarks somewhere that all facts and personages of great importance in the world

occur, as it were, twice. He forgot to add: the first time as tragedy, the second as farce.' (Karl Marx, *The Eighteenth Brumaire of Louis Bonaparte*, 1851.)

In a television interview recorded shortly before his death, the Russian film-maker Andrei Tarkovsky repeated the maxim that the artist exists because the world is not perfect. The original *Utopia* was written by Thomas More partly to suggest what was amiss in the state of England (it was first published in 1516 in Leiden). 'Utopia' is literally 'the ideal nowhere', a theme that was more sympathetically continued, towards the end of the nineteenth century, in William Morris's romance *News from nowhere*. The fallibility of human nature, accepted as a premiss by conservatives, was ignored by Karl Marx's historical materialism and by the Bolsheviks. Their attempt, in the name of the proletariat, to bypass the bourgeois epoch and kick-start a massive industrial revolution, only resulted in a sharing of scarcity. After Stalin's death the grim joke emerged: 'Question: "Is it possible to build socialism in one country?" Answer: "Yes, but it should be somebody else's."'

It was the energetic, wealthy, but morally conscious protestant traders of the Netherlands, living in a fragile topography, who laid the base for the particular balance of individualism and collective responsibility, which still allows glimpses of a better world. An example from present-day Holland: the Wibaut prize for social housing is named in memory of the Amsterdam councillor who (from 1914) fought for high standards of housing.

Utopia, by its very nature, will always be elusive and fragmentary. But a spirit of hope and a refusal to accept conservative resignation to the idea that the present state of affairs cannot be improved and that human nature will never change: these are the things that provide the radical, utopian impulse. The evolving, complex history of the modern project continues, contradicting the simplicities of the soundbite. Now it is not the cultural radicals who inspire, but rather the productive avant-garde, with its idealism and sense of continuity.

Sea and Ships pavilion, Skylon and the Dome of Discovery. (From: Mary Banham & Bevis Hillier, *A tonic to the nation*, 1976)

The Netherlands: the model republic

It's progress if you can stop the world slipping away.
My humble model for progress is the reclamation of land.
Which is repeatedly, never-endingly retrieving what is lost.
A dogged and vigilant business...
    Graham Swift:
    Waterland, 1983

De Dageraad and De Stijl

Michel de Klerk's Eigen Haard housing and post office in Amsterdam (1917–20). Photographed in 1996

Like Venice, Amsterdam was a merchant city standing in water; but as a model bourgeois republic it was an impressive city of houses, not palaces. The high cost of pile foundations gave rise to the particular style of cross-walled, narrow-fronted dwellings, the shared cost of the party walls another example of Dutch co-operation. This, together with the confidence and self-reliance of individual world-wide traders, helped form a distinctive architecture with a strong sense of community. The system of construction, with load taken on the cross walls, left the front and end walls free to be treated as a light timber framework, with large areas of glazing: an early example of the 'free façade', which would become one of Le Corbusier's 'five points of a new architecture'. The frame and single-skin brick infill, sometimes expressed as decoration by the bonded patterning, was treated with linseed oil, to keep out the damp: giving a shiny, ship-like feeling.

By the 1920s, within the context of Berlage's plan for South Amsterdam, the marine metaphor for ship and furrow is expressed by the brick prow-like roofline of P.L. Kramer's corner building for the Dageraad ('dawn') housing block for the socialist housing association of the same name: a joint commission with the more ebullient Michel de Klerk, in this instance remarkably restrained. Architects of the Amsterdam School had often been called in to produce acceptable façades over standard plans, in order to obtain approval from the public committee (reputedly at a standard fee per metre, regardless of height), and this led to the epithet 'pinafore architecture'. However, De Klerk and Kramer were responsible for all aspects of this design, which was built with council subsidy, satisfying all the local requirements. The marked improvement in living standards and the great attention given to the exterior was fought for by the socialist Alderman Wibaut, in the face of accusations of extravagance and unneccessary elaboration of the façades. In his honour, a bust features on one of the curved corners.

J.J.P. Oud's 1924 housing at the Hook of Holland shares a similar social programme, as well as a predilection for curved form. But here the marine imagery is brought up to date. As a city architect in the more industrial port of Rotterdam, Oud helped to create a more functional ethos, in opposition to the Amsterdam School. This was marked by the formation of the 'Opbouw' group in 1920; a similar functionalist group 'De 8' was formed in Amsterdam in 1927. Oud was also associated, at its outset, with the Stijl group, though not signing any of the manifestos. Café De Unie in Rotterdam, designed by him in 1925 and reconstructed in 1985 on a nearby site, is a typical composition of balanced asymmetry using the primary colours which were the hallmark of De Stijl: red, yellow and blue, albeit fronting a pretty ordinary plan.

The 2 cent 1924 life-saving service stamp designed by P.A.H. Hofman, on the post-card of the Dageraad, depicting a stormy sea-tossed sailing ship, fits perfectly with the aesthetic of the Amsterdam School

The 8½ cent red and
6 cent green stamps
were also designed
by P.L. Kramer: part
of a seaman's fund
set of 1933, showing
a project monument
and lifeboat respec-
tively. The 1946 1½
cent by H. Levign for
the War Victims Relief
Fund – an emblem of
abundance (including
tulips!) – marked a
return to traditional
engraving. The let-
tering is by the master
typographer, Jan van
Krimpen

Domesticity in the model republic

Uniquely in the Netherlands, architectural development was closely followed by postal design: largely due to the efforts of J.F. van Royen. Joining the Dutch Post Office (PTT) in 1904, his first success came only in 1913, when he managed to persuade the board to accept a design by K.P.C. de Bazel, an old pupil of Berlage. This was for the independence centenary issue: royal portraits in tapestry-like frames with a geometric basis that anticipates De Stijl. It marked a turning point for Dutch stamps, and other remarkable designs followed, reflecting the spirit of the times, from Art Nouveau and Expressionism to the radical photomontages of the 1930s. Michel de Klerk and P.L. Kramer, the best-known architects of the Amsterdam School, were among those contributing designs

Vermeer's *Street in Delft* remains a favourite image of many architects, with its combination of strong horizontal and vertical features, front and back – or, rather – side views, formal and informal elements, and especially the threshold between the home and the world. A front and side door, their relative importance marked by similar raising and lowering of scale, and even the little bench under the window, appear again in the Schröder house of Gerrit Rietveld in 1924. For the Schröder children playing on the threshold, there was even a little hatch inside the front door, to pop their toys in. The red blouse and blue apron of the washerwoman match the back and seat plane of the 'red-blue' chair by Rietveld.

This chair was originally designed in 1918, the colours being added subsequently to bring it into line with De Stijl's canon of the three primary colours. It also demonstrated other De Stijl theoretical concerns: the implied continuity of space, dematerialized coloured planes, and a modular system of standard sections, machine-cut but hand-assembled in traditional peg-and-nail construction, meant for economy as a bridge between machine and hand craft. But for all this, as Rietveld himself admitted, it was not especially comfortable, and the square ends were a definite injury hazard. The bright colours helped to offset the distinctly puritan air.

H.P. Berlage's Amsterdam Stock Exchange of 1893–1903, with its un-plastered brickwork and absolute clarity of structural expression, remains a masterpiece of its time. With such work, together with his championing of Frank Lloyd Wright and his idealistic socialism, Berlage can be seen as pointing the way for a socially committed modern architecture. 'The art of the master-builder lies in this: the creation of space, not the sketching of façades. A spatial envelope is established by means of walls, whereby a space or series of spaces is manifested, according to the complexity of the walling.' Writing in 1908, he further insists that the wall should both plain and plane. This, together with an overriding emphasis on the 'unity in plurality' of proportional systems could lead, he believed, to repose or style,

clearly pointing towards the later school of De Stijl. But whereas the space Berlage admired so much in Wright – the Larkin Building of 1903, especially – and which he demonstrated in the Stock Exchange – remained primarily contained within the building envelope, De Stijl strove toward a more extensive continuum. Berlage's wall planes too have a distinctly substantive quality, rather than the apparently dematerialized floating planes of De Stijl compositions such as Van Doesburg's (which remained unbuilt). The juxtaposition of this solidity with the light metal trusses and patent glazing, the tough and the delicate, is carried on in the more clearly modern style of the Gemeentemuseum in The Hague, his last work and a superb testament: from the majestic scale of the entry hall down to the exquisite detail of the beautifully lit display cabinets that can be seen projecting from the subtly bonded brick-facing wall surface.

From the serene, reticent art of Vermeer and the beautifully observed domesticity of Pieter de Hooch, via the unadorned planes of H.P. Berlage's architecture, to the aesthetic of De Stijl and the moral force of constructivism, there remained an underlying consistency of development that reflected the social programme of this model republic.

The art of the master builder: Berlage's Gemeentemuseum in The Hague (designed 1927–9). Photographed in 1996

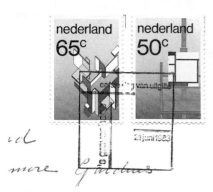

De Stijl was commemorated by the PTT in 1983 with two stamps by Wim Crouwel, based on designs by Mondrian and Van Doesburg in the three primary colours, completed with a square first-day postmark

Vilmos Huszàr,
*Composition 2:
the ice-skaters* (1917).
(Gemeentemuseum,
The Hague)

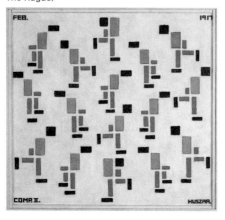

Holland had been fortunate in not being drawn into the industrialized mass destruction that was the First World War; the curtailed economy meant few buildings, but more time for theoretical exploration. Robert van 't Hoff, however, had in 1916 managed to complete his first concrete-framed house, clearly influenced by Wright, at Huis ter Heide, near Utrecht. The painter Piet Mondrian had returned from Paris in 1914. Already in 1917, his style evolved into horizontal and vertical elements alone, in parallel with Huszàr and Van der Leck. The ground was prepared for the emergence of De Stijl.

Never a homogenous group or 'ism', but more a loose collective around the magazine of the same name, published by Theo van Doesburg, De Stijl existed from 1917 to 1931. The magazine's first cover was designed by Vilmos Huszàr, whose wittily abstracted skaters were also painted in 1917. The De Stijl manifesto was not spelled out until 1918, by which time Van Doesburg published the magazine himself, with financial support from Van 't Hoff. J.J.P. Oud and Gerrit Rietveld, original members, did not sign, and the painter Bart van der Leck had already left. Robert van 't Hoff withdrew his support in 1919, and with the radical re-design by Mondrian and Van Doesburg of 1921, Huszàr cancelled his subscription. Nevertheless, this cover was an early example of what came to be known as the New Typography that could be seen in avant-garde publications through Russia and Europe: a definite advance.

Rietveld's buffet of 1919, an elaboration of the principles demonstrated in the red-blue chair, appears more obviously architectonic. Its articulation of frame and infill looked back to the timber-framed houses and forward to a similar handling of the service pods in Richard Rogers' Lloyd's building of 1986.

W.M. Dudok's Dr H. Bavinckschool of 1921–2 is a typical example of this Hilversum architect's unique synthesis of the best of tradition with Amsterdam School architecture, and including elements of De Stijl. The smaller tower fits the compositional massing, marking the entrance, more comfortably than the overwhelming tower of the more

famous and superb Town Hall of 1924–30.

As a young man, the high-born Van 't Hoff had been inspired by the 'Walden' commune in Bussum, and he continued in England with studies of such utopian societies, first at the Birmingham School of Art, then at the Architectural Association in London, subsequently building a studio for Augustus John in Chelsea. After a visit to the USA, where he met Frank Lloyd Wright and received a copy of the first Wasmuth edition of Wright's works, he returned to Holland, designing the Villa Henny (at Huis ter Heide) in 1914. With the failure of his dreams of a socialist Europe, Van 't Hoff retired from public life, settling finally in England, on the edge of the New Forest, in 1937. He died in 1979.

↗
The 75 cent airmail from 1928 is by Chris Lebeau, celebrating one of the pioneers of Dutch aviation, A.N.J. Tomassen à Thuessink van der Hoop (luckily his name did not have to be included in the design), who flew the first mails to the Dutch East Indies in 1924

→
1969 saw the Villa Henny celebrated on a 12 cent summer charity issue. Hopefully somebody sent Van 't Hoff a card

NEDERLAND
75 Cᴱᴺᵀ LUCHTPOST

NEDERLAND

DE STIJL
ND

VIJFDE JAARGANG 1922

9

WEIMAR
HAAG ANTWERPEN PARIJS ROME

INTERNATIONAAL MAANDBLAD
VOOR NIEUWE KUNST WETEN-
SCHAP EN KULTUUR REDACTIE
THEO VAN DOESBURG

12 +8 C
NEDERLAND

DW 95

J.J.P. Oud's Kiefhoek terrace houses, Rotterdam (designed 1925). Photographed in 1975

The 'Tachtigers' ('eighty-ers') were a radical literary group led by the poet Willem Kloos between 1880 and 1889. Their philosophy was of an art divorced from society: the antithesis of the later De Stijl movement, which was still condemning these Tachtigers some forty years later. Nevertheless, one Tachtiger, Herman Gorter, moved on from individualism to become a fierce propagandist for the Dutch Social Democratic Workers' Party, before helping to found the Dutch Communist Party. Meanwhile, Christiaan Marie Emil Küpper, on border duty with the Dutch army bicycle brigade, had met with Piet Mondrian, Bart van der Leck and J.J.P. Oud, who all shared his utopian views on art and architecture. Adopting the name Theo van Doesburg, he founded the magazine *De Stijl* in 1917. For all the radicalism of its first manifesto in 1918, Van Doesburg remained steadfastly apolitical.

'There is an old and a new consciousness of time. The old is connected with the individual. The new is connected with the universal. The struggle of the individual against the universal reveals itself both in the world struggle as well as in the art of our time.'

'The artists of today have been driven the whole world over by the same consciousness, and therefore have taken part from an intellectual point of view in this war against the domination of individual despotism. They therefore sympathize with all who work for the formation of an international unity in life, art, culture, either intellectually or materially.'

Jan Wils and Robert van 't Hoff, who had produced key buildings published in *De Stijl*, were both communists. They took the use of the word 'struggle' to have political weight. When the Dutch government, together with other European powers, put a ban on post to and from Russia, they were among a group of artists that petitioned the government to lift the ban. Van Doesburg, with all his foreign contacts, was also supposed to lobby for them to petition. His failure to do this prompted Wils and Van 't Hoff to leave the group. J.J.P. Oud, by now principal housing architect for the city of Rotterdam, was busy producing housing at the Hook of Holland and in Rotterdam at Kiefhoek. Here a fine balance between the universal – the treatment of façades as part of the whole urban fabric – and the secondary articulation of individual units, made an exemplary fusion of functional economy and artistry. The primary colours are used on window, door and railings. At Kiefhoek, with 300 units, two shops and a laundry, Oud entered a zero-fee bid on the church, to preserve the unity of design. Van Doesburg was contemptuous, particularly of the circular ends. This finalized Oud's break with De Stijl.

The Opbouw collective, with Piet Zwart as president, provided a much better context for Oud's more functionalist objectives. It then merged with the eight of Amsterdam, to form 'De 8 en Opbouw', the most important architectural grouping of the period. Among its members were Van Loghem, Van der Vlugt, Bijvoet, Duiker, Cor van Eesteren, Rietveld, Mart Stam, J.G. Wiebenga and Jan Wils.

J.J.P. Oud's design for the Congress building, The Hague, concluded this memorable set issued in 1969, designed by R.J. Draijer

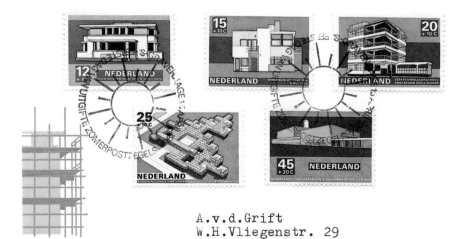

A.v.d.Grift
W.H.Vliegenstr. 29
Dordrecht

LS 1969

RST DAY OF ISSUE

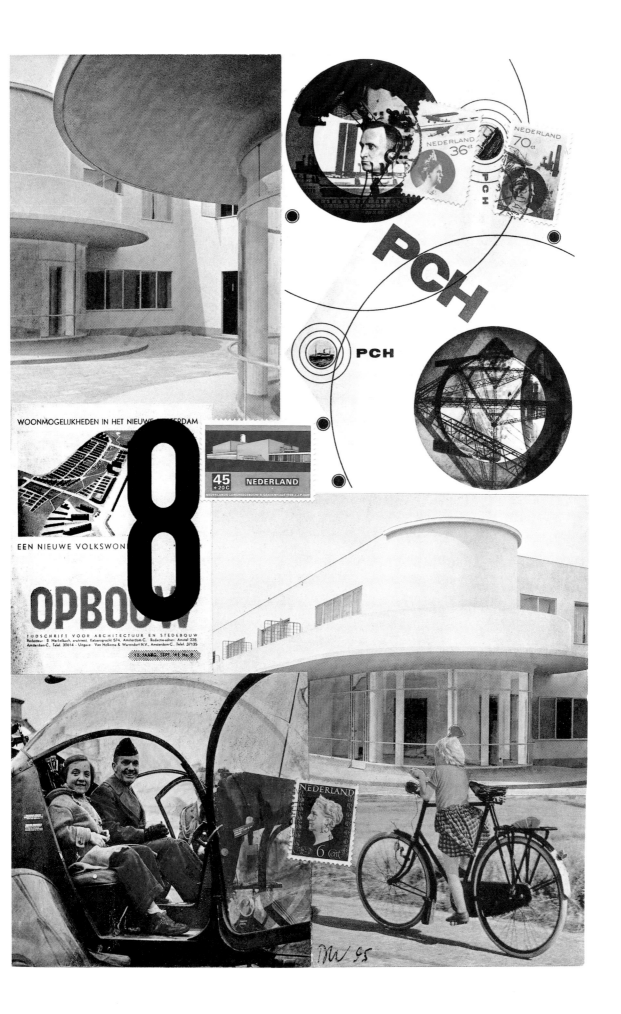

Odd that Van Doesburg's universalism eschewed the circle. *Circle* was even the title chosen for the first 'international survey of constructive art', published in London in 1937. Edited by Leslie Martin, Ben Nicholson and Naum Gabo, this ground-breaking collection included articles by Le Corbusier, Mondrian, Moholy-Nagy and Jan Tschichold. And for Piet Zwart, the architect and typographer ('typotect'), whose symbol was the letter P and a black ('zwart') square, circular form was a favourite, used on all his stamp designs and many posters. Zwart had worked for both Jan Wils and Berlage before meeting El Lissitzky and Kurt Schwitters in 1923. El Lissitzky gave him a copy of Mayakovsky's *For the voice*, which set him on the path of typography.

Another Russian image forms the backdrop here: Aleksandr Rodchenko's photomontage of Osip Brik, with the masthead of *LEF* magazine drawn over one lense. Zwart, Gerard Kiljan and Paul Schuitema, became the key Dutch designers using photomontage. In 1931–2 they were each commissioned by J.F. van Royen to produce stamp designs for the PTT. Schuitema, a promising young artist in the 1920s, abandoned painting for graphic design and photography, working with the worker-photographers' movement and *Links Richten* magazine. Piet Zwart's 70 cent, 80 cent, and 36 cent airmail were standard isssues, in an A11 format to the new German (DIN)

standard paper sizes. Zwart designed stamps to be part of a whole, together with the postmark and address on the envelope. His systematic approach to design led Hannes Meyer to invite him to teach at the Bauhaus in 1931.

Gerard Kiljan's dramatically stark and unsentimental portraits of disabled children on the charity issues of 1931 marked the introduction of 'nieuwe zakelijkheid' through the letterbox. ('Nieuwe zakelijkheid': the Dutch equivalent of 'Neue Sachlichkeit', or functional matter-of-factness.) The particular Dutch concern for children is reflected in the PTT's many charity stamps. It is interesting to compare this issue of 1931 with the growing Nazi attitude in Germany at that time: with the eminent poet Gottfried Benn advocating the purification of the body politic rather than waste resources on handicapped children.

The championing by Van Royen at the PTT of such radical designers alongside more traditional approaches, led to complaints of state-supported anarchy. Retrenchment followed, before the abrupt halt of 1940, when the Nazis invaded the Netherlands.

Stamp and PTT advertisement by Piet Zwart, seen as a mail shot

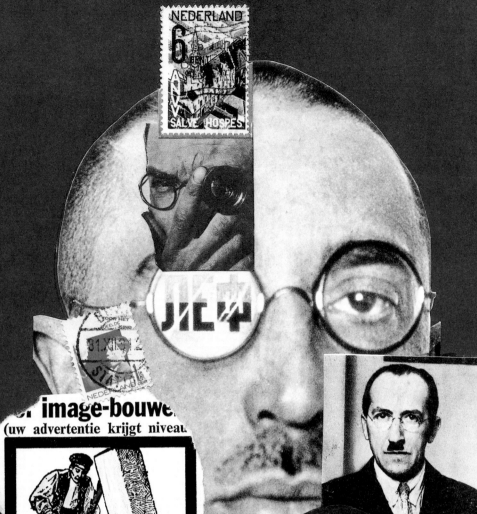

The two row houses in
Utrecht, by Rietveld
and Schröder
(1930–1), across
the road from Mrs
Schröder's house.
Photographed in 1963

'Under the pavement, the beach'. This
slogan, from the Situationists during
the 1968 uprising in Paris, is literally
the case in Holland, where 40 per cent
of the country lies below sea level.
The Netherlands, indeed.

At the time of its construction,
the tiny Schröder house – it would
fit into the living room of Frank Lloyd
Wright's Robie house – marked the
end of a terrace and of the town, looking over open country and with a canal
and pond in the back garden. A subsequent ring-road destroyed the idyll,
even prompting Rietveld to sugggest
demolition.

By 1963 (the time of the photograph, left), work was starting on
the extension and raising of this road,
which by then was the site of two later
sets of row houses, in the new building
style of the 1930s: the first designed
again in collaboration with Mrs
Schröder. Rietveld, the innovator,
had moved on.

The founding of Leiden University in
1575 was seen as a cultural declaration
of independence and Janus Dousa the
elder, its first curator, was the epitome
of patriotic scholarship. In 1574 the
siege of Leiden by the Spanish had
been lifted only by breaching the sea
dykes, which impeded the invading
troops. Leiden and Utrecht were the
first university towns, and in 1917 it
was Van Doesburg and Oud, both then
living in Leiden, who founded De Stijl.
This centre of scholarship was also
the centre of commerce, and the first
'futures' market could be said to have
come into its own, with disastrous con-
sequences, in the great tulip specula-
tion of 1636–7. Hardly a staple
commodity, originally imported from
Turkey, the tulip above other flowers
became an obvious sign of conspic-
uous consumption, whether in the soil
or on canvas. At the height of his De
Stijl abstraction, Piet Mondrian would
even resort to flower painting to make
ends meet. In the famous photograph
of his studio, taken by André Kertész
in 1926, the tulips are painted all over
white; with anger possibly?

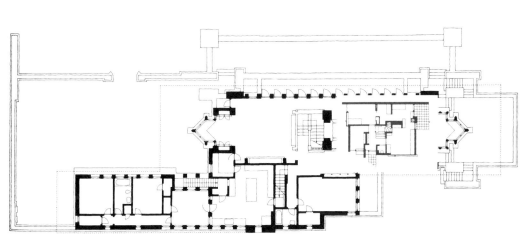

The Schröder house (in red) shown to same scale as the Robie house. (From: David Dunster, *Key buildings of the twentieth century*, 1985)

The milkmaid by Jan
Vermeer (1658–60).
(Rijksmuseum,
Amsterdam)

The poetically observed domesticity
of a Vermeer painting becomes in the
Schröder house a constructed elaboration of homely functionalism. Like
Vermeer's interiors, the first floor is
flooded with light; the substantial
transom is now used for roller blinds
to shield the lower casement; where
before there were shutters, producing
a variation in light that was used to
dramatic effect. There's a fine descrip-
tion of this in Steen Eiler Rasmussen's
book *Experiencing architecture*. For
some reason, Mrs Schröder did not
care for high ceilings, so the spatial
effect is more horizontal, akin to
Frank Lloyd Wright's houses.

This compact house carries the
Wrightian idea of the dissolution of the
box even further, with the completely
open corner formed by the two adja-
cent side-hung casements. Together
with the cantilevered roof plane, this
sense of visual expansion to command
the outside space compensates for
the relatively shallow internal space.
Furniture, fittings, colour, and architecture are brought together by the
cabinet-maker Rietveld in this masterpiece of De Stijl. Modest in scale and
materials, yet priceless, it also seems a
typical example of what Simon Schama
termed 'the embarrassment of riches',
as in the title of his definitive study of
Dutch culture.

The minimal planning of sleeping
cabins praised by Le Corbusier in *Vers
une architecture* is followed here with
the arrangement of sliding partitions
that would divide bedroom and bath-
room spaces for night-time. Mrs
Schröder's bedroom is little more than
a cupboard in this arrangement. For
the children it must have been difficult
at times, putting up with the taunts
of classmates and living with such
an elaborately constructed order
and its necessary regime of tidiness.
The zig-zag chair is another example
of Rietveld's great inventiveness. This
was always manually evolved, from
little paper and card models.

Van Doesburg had sent Rietveld
a postcard, hoping that he might be
involved as a painter, but the building
itself became the painting, and indeed
no paintings were ever hung: just the
occasional photograph or print. The
extraordinary Mrs Schröder, who left
her husband to live here with her three
children, stayed until her death in 1985
(aged 96). For the last years of his life,
Rietveld himself moved in. Clearly this
was an exceptional meeting of minds.

Outside the window, Rietveld
standing behind the stable door detail,
is the towering figure of the young
Mart Stam and the diminutive prophet
of the new architecture of world revolution, El Lissitzky.

←↗
Paul Schuitema's
collage design is one
of a set of stamps
promoting tourism:
a reminder of the
house's status, now
recognized as a
museum piece. In
a way it always was
that

The headquarters building of the Dutch Trading Company in Amsterdam was K.P.C. de Bazel's last building. The company had been set up for colonial trade by King Willem I, whose portrait featured on De Bazel's stamp design of 1913. What worked graphically at the smaller scale is less successful as a monumental layering of brick and stone – covering a concrete frame only expressed internally with two light courts that have since been filled in. Dating from 1919–26, it seemed already old-fashioned when compared with the developments of De Stijl, the Hook of Holland housing by J.J.P. Oud, or Dudok's early work in Hilversum.

Sailing in on a fresh ideological breeze is the Bergpolder apartment block, of 1933–4, by Van Tijen, Brinkman and Van der Vlugt. Coming after the Van Nelle factory of 1925–31, it confirmed the presence of the 'nieuwe zakelijkheid'. The building was extensively covered in Alfred Roth's *The new architecture*. This historic book, designed by Max Bill and first published in 1940, was the definitive catalogue of this approach to architecture. It remains unsurpassed in its clarity of presentation, from intention to constructional detail.

The Bergpolder flats can be seen as a prototype for the now largely discredited access balcony slab blocks. However, in the case of this block, still in use today, albeit with enlarged rooms, the vertical is compensated for by the lower block and communal services. This both helps the transition from street scale, while sheltering the large south-west facing communal garden and nursery. The original purpose was to provide low-cost workers' housing, being built by the M.B.H. Volkswoningbouw Rotterdam construction company, using prefabrication and standardization as much as possible: a light-weight braced steel structure with alternating concrete and timber flooring did prove economic, but a little too elastic. After the maintenance problems of the zinc sprayed steel facing panels and the lack of privacy with continuous balconies, Van Tijen's second version of the form, Plaslaan of 1937–8, was constructed in concrete, with deeper, separate balconies. The Bergpolder slab was also the first to use lift access – a large open cab stopping at alternate half-landings. A refuse chute was placed outside the centre of the east-facing access balcony, while the west side was fitted with adjustable sunscreens. An odd anomaly was that these remained cold-water flats. Hot water had to be collected from the laundry or the caretaker. Dutch puritanism meets economic expediency.

↗→
The different treatments of Queen Wilhelmina's portrait follow the rationalizing trend of the architecture: starting with De Bazel's 10 cent design for the centenary of Dutch independence; Piet Zwart's 80 cent photomontage of 1931 – the first of its type, and in this case a mint specimen is highly valued; and the 1½ cent of 1938, part of a set issued for her anniversary

Brinkman & Van der Vlugt's Van Nelle factory, Rotterdam (1925–31). Photographed in 1991

Enlightened functionalism

Mercury, the winged messenger and guardian deity of commerce, looks down on the first phase of the ground-breaking Van Nelle factory (1925–31) in this finely engraved 1929 air mail by Jac Jongert, the principal advertising designer for Van Nelle from 1919 to 1940. The ascendant middle class and traders of the 1648 republic tempered their new-found wealth with a concern for order and cleanliness that was as much literal as spiritual. Pieter de Hooch's celebration of clean linen features a bronze figure of Mercury standing guard over the threshold – a Dutch version of Feng Shui perhaps. This use of deep perspective space to evoke the relationship between home and the world was used to great effect by Jean Renoir in the film *Boudu sauvé des eaux* ('Boudu saved from drowning'), which poked fun at such bourgeois values. For the dominant class cleanliness was next to godliness and the passion for a humane order is the thread that runs through to the present.

Built on a sandy polder, next to the water, albeit on substantial piled foundations, the Van Nelle factory could be seen, as here, standing on the spiritual base implied by Pieter Saenredam's *Interior of St. Adolphus* of 1649. Saenredam was unique in his time for portraying such calm architectural order with absolute clarity, and the subtle but vibrant colouring emphasized the spatial architectonics.

The firm of Van Nelle, whose products were the staples of tobacco, coffee, tea, had been owned by the Van der Leeuw family since 1837. But it was the young Kees van der Leeuw, an original member of the theosophical Order of the Star in the East, who already in 1914 started on the idea of a new factory. By the 1920s, a profound shift away from the values of mystical geometry toward a clearer functionalism had even occured in theosophical circles – so much so that by 1929 Krishnamurti had dissolved the Order of the Star in the East. Kees van der Leeuw had travelled to the USA to study the most advanced examples of factory organization and management, so that the principles of Taylorism and the example of Henry Ford could be incorporated – but with much greater concern for the workers themselves.

In this brave new factory Kees van der Leeuw can be seen to follow the example of Robert Owen, the early utopian socialist factory owner, but taking full advantage of the most advanced techniques of management and construction. The logic of this construction, with its tapering mushroom columns, flat edge cantilevered concrete slab and curtain wall, mark it as the most advanced building of its type, following the line of Le Corbusier's 'Dom-Ino' frame, Walter Gropius's Fagus factory of 1911, and of course the Bauhaus building at Dessau.

Brinkman & Van der Vlugt's team working on the Van Nelle factory included the exceptional Mart Stam, whose perspective drawing lacked the crowning curved turret, which he opposed. This, together with the suppression of his contribution, was said to have lead to his departure from the firm. A more fundamental split, however, was occuring between the old left, with its ethically tinged socialism, and the young communists inspired by the Russian revolution and the new credo of constructivism.

Disappointed when the workers at Van Nelle failed to live up to his idea of a model society, Van der Leeuw left to study with Freud and Adler in Vienna. In 1939 he returned to the board of Van Nelle and subsequent key governmental and curatorial roles.

Psychoanalysis would not be needed to understand that society could not be changed by good design alone, and the workers bathed in light, like the prisoners emerging from the dungeons in Beethoven's *Fidelio*, might be excused for not bursting into song, given the unchanged division of labour and productive relations. But what shines through still today in this exceptional building is its progressive idealism.

Pieter de Hooch's celebration of clean linen (*The linen cupboard*, 1663). (Rijksmuseum, Amsterdam)

↗
The fine engraving by F. Lammers, using an ochre similar to Saenredam's, on this 2+3 cent welfare issue of 1955 belongs to a set that included buildings by Berlage, Dudok and Oud

Leen van der Vlugt

Successful 'streets in the air' at Spangen in Rotterdam, built in 1920 and still in use. Photographed in 1975

Leen van der Vlugt stands alongside his Amilcar 8, for which he designed the leather-clad body work. The curved forms of the Sonneveld staircase and the roof of the tennis club – featured in *Circle* (1937), the first substantial publication of the new art and architecture in England – distanced him from the harder line of his co-designer on the Van Nelle factory, Mart Stam. Stam's brilliant early career had included working in Berlin with Hans Poelzig and Max Taut, and in Zurich with Werner Moser, publishing *ABC* with Hans Schmidt and Emil Roth, before joining Brinkman & Van der Vlugt and the Opbouw group. Mies van der Rohe invited him to build at the Weissenhof; he lectured at the Dessau Bauhaus and was a member of the Dutch delegation at the CIAM conference at La Sarraz, before spending four years in Russia with Ernst May, to build new towns such as Magnitogorsk.

The firm of Brinkman & Van der Vlugt was from its outset closely associated with Kees van der Leeuw of Van Nelle. It seems that the housing trust that commissioned Michiel Brinkman at Spangen was dominated by him. The fact remains that this pioneering scheme of 1919–22, with its wide access decks to the upper level remains the most succcessful example of 'streets in the air'. Its front doors and windows facing onto the gallery, which is open to the sky, are closer to street architecture than the faceless overshadowed decks of the Parkhill estate at Sheffield.

In 1920 Brinkman & Van der Vlugt designed a prismatic, modern summerhouse for Krishnamurti, whose meetings they attended together with Van der Leeuw. In the tennis club, the exposed steel framing that punches through the roof canopy over the projecting bay is a similar device to that used in the 1929 house for Van der Leeuw, which was far more literally a 'machine for living in', with its sliding systems and multiple appliances, than any of Le Corbusier's houses. Richard Neutra, who had stayed there, was both impressed and greatly influenced by its design, which has been claimed for Mart Stam. Van der Leeuw himself, however, credited Van der Vlugt; he had also brought ideas and equipment from the USA. It was only lived in for

three years before he left for Vienna, and is now a gentleman's club. Van der Vlugt's remaining designs, before his death in 1936, included the exposed steel framed Feyenoord football stadium and the Dutch standard telephone kiosk of 1932.

↗
The 1928 Olympic stamp, designed by L.O. Wenckenbach, fits well with the 'nieuwe bouwen' spirit

De Volharding's glass architecture

The social-democrat architect J.W.E. Buijs, together with J.B. Lürsen, produced the first glass masterpiece for the working class, the headquarters of the Volharding ('perseverance') co-operative society. This was a true collective organization offering a variety of services, and its architectural expression now seems an embodiment of Paul Scheerbart and Bruno Taut's utopian dreams of 'Glasarchitektur'. Taut's little glass pavilion at Cologne in 1914 had been a forerunner of the crystal-like beacon to the future shown in Lyonel Feininger's famous woodcut for the first Bauhaus proclamation in 1919, heralding a new society. For Scheerbart and Taut, in particular, the transparency of glass was symbolic both of purity and an open society, its apparent weightlessness an allegory of liberation. (With the arrival of reflective glass, this utopian vision would undergo an inversion, to become realized as corporate nightmare.)

The diffusing glass spandrel panels of the Volharding façade projected 70cm, allowing access behind for a system of lettering not unlike that used on cinemas, to make this a variable, graphic, 'architecture parlante'; as suggested by such constructivist projects as the Vesenin brothers' Pravda tower competition entry of 1924, with a similar propagandist aim. While the largely glass architecture of the Van Nelle factory and offices was lavishly praised, the hardliners of Dutch functionalism were critical of Buijs's perceived eclecticism. J.B. van Loghem referred to it as 'still decorative'. This was in his seminal *Bouwen* (1932), the textbook of 'nieuwe zakelijkheid', designed by Paul Schuitema.

Meanwhile in Moscow, the Central Union of Consumer Co-operatives (Centrosoyuz) were to have their headquarters designed by Le Corbusier. Finally completed in 1936, seven years after the first design, it too had a wide glazed spandrel. Whereas in the Volharding this diaphragm was exploited for advertising, the workers of Narkomlegprom – state industries had replaced co-operatives – would find this space useful for keeping their groceries fresh in the Moscow winter.

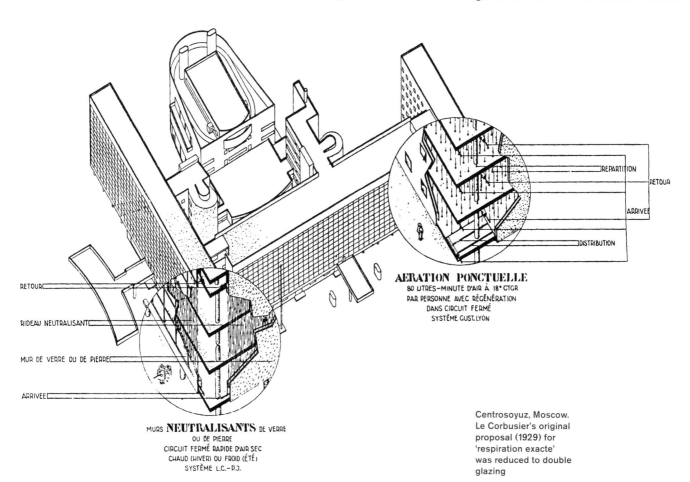

AÉRATION PONCTUELLE
80 LITRES-MINUTE D'AIR À 18° CTGR
PAR PERSONNE AVEC RÉGÉNÉRATION
DANS CIRCUIT FERMÉ
SYSTÈME GUST. LYON

REPARTITION
RETOUR
ARRIVÉE
DISTRIBUTION

RETOUR
RIDEAU NEUTRALISANT
MUR DE VERRE OU DE PIERRE
ARRIVÉE

MURS **NEUTRALISANTS** DE VERRE
OU DE PIERRE
CIRCUIT FERMÉ RAPIDE D'AIR SEC
CHAUD (HIVER) OU FROID (ÉTÉ)
SYSTÈME L.C.-P.J.

Centrosoyuz, Moscow.
Le Corbusier's original
proposal (1929) for
'respiration exacte'
was reduced to double
glazing

Johannes Duiker's
Cineac cinema,
Amsterdam (1933–4).
Photographed in 1976

'Bouwkundig ingenieur'

A fully-fledged constructivism arrived in Amsterdam with Bijvoet & Duiker's open air school of 1927–30. This muscular doctrine of radical social programme within a clearly expressed structural frame was first articulated by Aleksei Gan in Soviet Russia and quickly spread to radical groups throughout Europe. The romance of flight and technology of aircraft design expressed by Le Corbusier continued with Moisei Ginzburg's *Style and epoch*, published in Moscow in 1924, with the Caproni triplane featured on the title page: slightly more substantial than the glider in Lartigue's earlier photograph, taken at Château de Rouzat in 1909.

Johannes Duiker and Bernard Bijvoet both graduated from the Technische Hogeschool in Delft as 'bouwkundig ingenieur'. This title and qualification made a clear distinction with the then greater artistic pretension implied by the title 'architect'. The designs for this school, together with the technical school in Scheveningen, the Zonnestraal sanitorium, Cineac newsreel cinema and the Grand-Hotel Gooiland in Hilversum, remain the major works of this approach.

Situated in the heart of Berlage's South Amsterdam plan, the designs for the school met with considerable opposition from the predominantly expressionist Amsterdam School architects. It was only finally realized by partly concealing it within a perimeter block; so the multi-storey arrangement helped lift it out of potential winter shading. The economic cantilevered framework, including sheer profiled beams, further accentuated the light airy aesthetic. In the damp Netherlands, the detail of curving metal rod coat-hooks around the heating pipes was typical of Duiker's attention to detail, combining function with great elegance. The main heating system, however, proved unsuccessful; and, as with all Duiker's buildings, the external materials did not always perform as hoped. This was especially so with the now mainly abandoned Zonnestraal buildings, which certainly have not met with the classicists' demand for beautiful ruins. While the schools and sanitorium were concrete structures, the Cineac newsreel cinema and the last, posthumous work of the

Grand-Hotel Gooiland, were steel-framed, making full use of contemporary possibilities. Duiker even compared the Cineac to a flying machine. Taking full advantage of its corner site with superb interaction of curved and orthogonal forms – the curves of the Amsterdam School meet the straight lines of 'De 8 en Opbouw' – this little gem was a wonderful sight: especially at night, with its glazed projection booth and colourful vertical signs. Duiker's tragically premature death in 1935 spared him at least from the nightmares that were to follow.

Duiker's Zonnestraal,
Hilversum, with Julia
Bloomfield.
Photographed in 1963

Concrete socialism

Betendorp restored,
with external insulation
added. Photographed
in 1996

Beyond the edge of Berlage's South
Amsterdam plan, past the old Ajax
football stadium and allotment gardens, lies the Betendorp or 'concrete
village'. The built result of a competition for prefabricated housing types,
with ten final winning designs, it was
completed between 1921 and 1928.
A variety of approaches – from whole
wall elements to concrete block – and
styles – pitched or flat roofs, plain or
banded surfaces – are unified by the
same material, concrete; even more
so, now that all have been given a
necessary coat of insulation and
render to bring them up to standard.
The architects were J.B. van Loghem,
whose blocks are the plainest;
D. Greiner, who produced the master
plan and the centre shops, library and
meeting hall; W. Greve and J. Gratama.
In keeping with early socialist principles, no public drinking house was
permitted by the predominantly
communist and socialist tenants.
It was completed in time for the
1928 Olympics, which were held in
Amsterdam, on the other side of the
city, in Jan Wils's stadium, now the
home of F.C. Amsterdam. Ajax remain
the better team, however, and it was
the Betendorp that saw the birth of
Johan Cruyff, Holland's greatest
footballer. Where else but in the
Netherlands – with its football-pitch
landscape and the Dutch combination
of individualism and collective spirit –
could the concept of 'total football'
(interchangeable roles, a model of
democracy) have originated?

An early anti-alcohol
postcard: 'No more,
Dad!'

Ach Vader ! niet meer !

The first stamps issued under Nazi rule included this celebration of the Netherlands Legion of Volunteers. Others showed an idealized Aryan mother and child: an obscene parody of the Madonna, as Anne Frank and countless others were taken to their deaths

Whether the subsequent concept of 'total football' originated in the Netherlands or via the famed Hungarian army team led by Puskas, it certainly would not have been in the increasingly centralized Soviet Russia under Stalin, playing the paranoid defensive system; their brilliant but isolated striker Trotsky having been sent off in 1927. Politics out of sport? By 1930 the Graf Zeppelin was hovering over Wembley stadium – observing Arsenal's grim tactics, presumably. And by the time of the highly charged 1938 match in Berlin's Olympic Stadium, even the England team are forced to give the Nazi salute, which gives an idea of how far Neville Chamberlain's government was going with appeasement. England's first goal was greeted by a stunned silence. After a German equalizer, England went on to win 6–3.

The razing of Rotterdam by the Luftwaffe in 1940 began the Nazi invasion of the Netherlands. There had been no declaration of war, and large parts of Rotterdam were destroyed overnight. A Viennese lawyer was put in place as ruler of the country. The small Dutch Nazi party (about 80,000 members) gained prominence in the country. In 1942 the party's designer W.J.H. Nijs produced his first stamps, showing soldiers of the Netherlands legion – the pro-Nazi volunteers – of whom there were a surprising number. His blatant propagandist designs for the 1944 children's charity issue were in total contrast to Kiljan's. Designers such as Willem Sandberg and Mart Stam gave their skills to the resistance, forging ration books, stamps and identity cards. Several of these designers were imprisoned or shot. Zwart was taken hostage. And Van Royen himself died in the Amersfoort concentration camp in 1942.

Russia: what was to be done

All fixed, fast-frozen relations, with their train of ancient and venerable prejudices and opinions, are swept away, all new-formed ones become antiquated before they can ossify. All that is solid melts into air, all that is holy is profaned, and men at last are forced to face...the real condition of their lives and their relations with their fellow men.
Karl Marx & Friedrich Engels:
Communist manifesto, 1848

In the 1930s, the exploration and conquest of the vast frontier of Soviet sky was mirrored in the unique pictorial stamps of balloons and airships. In 1957 this boundary was crossed by Sputnik, the first orbiting satellite. The sky was not the limit

There's a lot of sky in Dutch landscape painting; but, in the vastness of the great Russian plain, the immensity of the sky above is overwhelming. Poised between Europe and Asia, the great Russian land mass became the stage for an even greater social transformation.

Well before the revolution there had been a tradition of artistic and political radicalism, proceeding hand in hand. Vladimir Tatlin's career was prototypical. He ran away from school to go to sea as a cabin boy, worked in an icon painting studio, before enrolling in 1902 (aged 17) at the Moscow College of Painting, Sculpture and Architecture, from where he was expelled in 1903. He finally received the 'certificate for professional draughtsmanship' from an art college in Penza, where he had been under surveillance for his activism following the 1905 revolution. During this time he sailed, and even worked as a boxer in the circus. By 1914 he was playing the bandore at the Russian exhibition of folk art in Berlin – and even before Kaiser Wilhelm, who complimented him. With the money earned, he travelled to Paris, met Picasso, and visited the Eiffel Tower – already the icon of a new engineering art.

One of the most familiar symbols of the revolution remains the spiral tower designed in 1919 by Vladimir Tatlin as a proposed monument to the Third International. This would have been among the many structures proposed under the banner of Lenin's plan for monumental propaganda. The model was constructed in the new 'Studio of Materials, Volume and Construction' in Petrograd, where Tatlin was professor. A collective, including students and colleagues Shapiro, Meerzon and Vinogradov constructed the amazing model from just two large-scale drawings. This model was then taken to Moscow for the eighth All-Russian Congress of Soviets in 1920. The same year, George Grosz and John Heartfield posed at the first international Dada exhibition in Berlin, with a placard stating that art was dead but the new machine art of Tatlin lived.

The monument has been reconstructed several times, most notably in 1925 for the Paris Exposition des Arts Décoratifs, alongside Melnikov's pavilion and Le Corbusier's Esprit Nouveau model apartment. While the latter was the subject of approbrium, the model of Tatlin's tower was awarded a gold medal. That year too, another, simplified model was paraded on May Day in Leningrad.

The European spirit of individualism would soon be subsumed within a regime of Asiatic collectivism, exemplified in the trajectory of Tatlin's career: the frail wings of his final project, a one-man flying machine, fluttering under an indifferent sky.

Aéroplane évoluant autour de la Tour Eiffel.

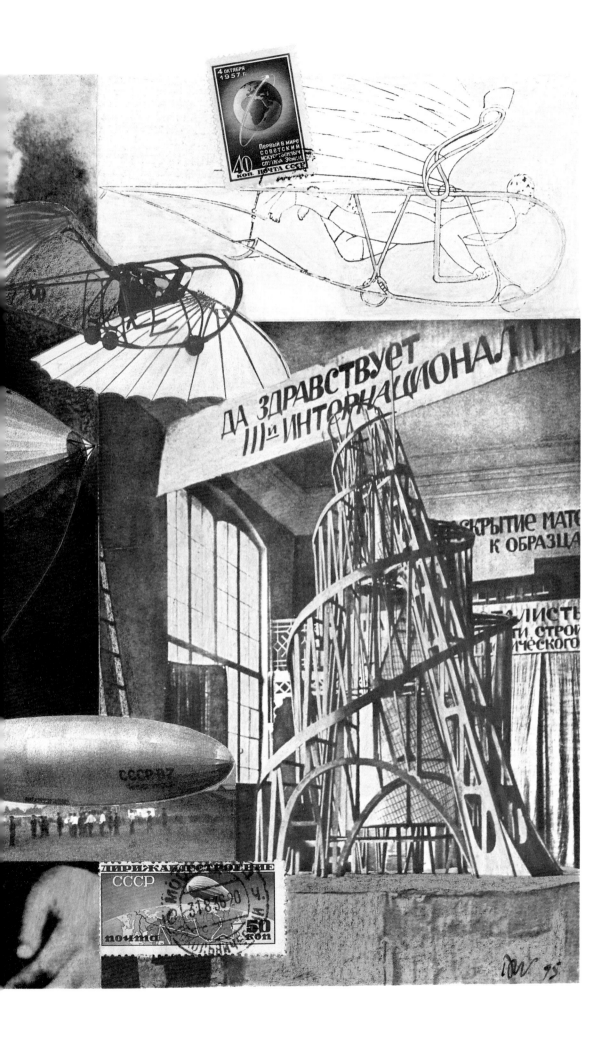

Rarely found used, the first post-revolutionary stamps, showing the shackles being severed by a modern Excalibur, were prepared under Kerensky's provisional government of February 1917, but not issued until 1918

'The fundamental and most stable feature of Russian history is the slow tempo of her development, with the economic backwardness, primitiveness of social forms and low level of culture resulting from it.'

The opening sentence of Leon Trotsky's classic history of the Russian revolution indicates the distance that separated Russia from Western Europe. Certainly the tiny Netherlands, with its progressive middle class, could not have been more different from the vast autocratic Russian empire, with its feeble bourgoisie.

Industrialization came late, and was government induced, with the resulting middle class cast more in the role of civil servants to the tsar than an independent political force; while the trade unions were founded and managed by the police. Social and political revolt, plots and assassinations, violence and repression marked a political heritage that sprang from a complete lack of open and legal debate about the major issues. The first mass uprising of 1905 was more a measure of weakness of the tsar at the narrow apex of this centralized power, than any co-ordinated political will. With the catastrophic losses of some eight million men in 1914–17, as poorly fed troops were thrown against the German lines, breaking point had been reached, and spontaneous revolution broke out in the cities in March 1917. Most of the revolutionary leaders were either in prison or in exile at the time. The German high command took a calculated risk in allowing Lenin and his circle back from Switzerland, in the famous sealed train to the Finland Station in Petrograd. His arrival provided the focus of political activism, which led to the Bolshevik seizure of power in October of that year.

The first attempt to overthrow the provisional government of 1917 had come from General Kornilov, the commander-in-chief of the tsarist forces, who marched on the capital with his supposedly loyal troops melting away behind him. This attempt, and the proposal to evacuate what had become the hotbed of revolution in Petrograd, ultimately swung popular opinion behind the Bolsheviks, and the initial seizure of power was an almost bloodless anti-climax: a seizure and occupa-

tion of key government buildings, one by one. The storming of the Winter Palace, the last redout of the provisional government, whose leader Kerensky had already made a tactical withdrawal in a limousine flying the American flag, was finally taken when shells were fired from the cruiser Aurora. But here, too, the popular image from documentary histories is an exaggerated fiction, taken from Eisenstein's film *October*.

In the comfortable headquarters of the occupied Smolny Institute, Lenin drafted the proclamation of Soviet power, on a page torn from an exercise book, and dated it 25 October 1917.

'The worker with a rifle, the bayonet above hat or cap, the rifle-belt over a civilian coat – that is the essential image of 25 October.'

(Trotsky)

Lenin in Red Square: the short-lived leader, destined to become a mummified icon, housed just a step away from this spot

In the White-controlled Ukraine, an archaic runic symbol was used to overprint, before their own issues were printed in 1918 and 1919. General Denikin escaped via France, and ended up in the USA. Admiral Kolchak was captured and shot in 1920; but General Yudenich, saved by the Allies, retired to England

Initial British support for the Whites would remain a bone of contention until the Second World War

The outpouring of creative energy that followed the October revolution was in direct proportion to the repression that had preceded it. The tension that had built up during the period of dual power (between the Soviets and the Duma or parliament) was released in a utopian euphoria. In the Netherlands, the manifesto of De Stijl, published as Lenin penned the Bolshevik proclamation of state power, seemed to give theoretical backing to the end of the bourgeois era. But where the sparse simplicity of De Stijl was aesthetic, poverty and shortage were the rule in Russia: here was the clean slate of modernism. Empty shop windows and even streets and squares were filled with posters and painted constructions. The Suprematist painter Nathan Altman designed the first major street art in Petrograd, for the first anniversary of the revolution, in 1918. His painting of 1920 gives an idea of the colours, while the winter-clad people give an idea of scale (20,000 arshins of canvas were used) and a reminder of the climate. There was no fuel available for studios, which kept the pace of work necessarily frenetic. A photograph of the Stenberg bothers' studio shows the spartan, modest means used to produce the striking posters for *October*, *Earth*, and many other films.

The low level of culture to which Trotsky referred was in marked contrast to the efforts of an artistic elite in the two main cities. After the 1905 revolution a radical modernism had flourished in Moscow and St Petersburg, with the patronage of a few progressive merchants, some of whom were also financing the revolutionary movement. Kasimir Malevich's suprematist compositions, Vladimir Tatlin's reliefs, Liubov Popova's paintings, and Vladimir Mayakovsky's poetry – *Cloud in trousers* was first read to Maxim Gorky in 1915 – were all seminal in the formation of an initial revolutionary, modernist culture. After the first flush of revolution in 1917, some patrons stayed to serve in Anatoly Lunacharsky's People's Commissariat of Enlightenment. One such figure was Aleksei Bakhrushin, founder of Moscow's first theatre museum, who would later be categorized as 'a class enemy of the worst kind' and written out of history.

The Stenberg brothers in their simply equipped studio

→
The tsar's government printing office was the best equipped of its day, and the 1913 Romanov dynasty commemorations, produced to compete with the Dutch issues by De Bazel, are superbly engraved. The tiny standard issues, with the double-headed eagle embossed, were rather brutally overprinted in 1922. This may have been expedient, but it could not have been more symbolic

↗→
Altman is credited with the Lenin mourning stamps of 1924: rather more traditional, but effective, compared with his constructivist design of 1922, which was not used

Following on from the Marxist slogan 'seriousness about science, ridicule of religion', the liberating potential of the machine was taken to the level of ideology by one group of socially minded designers: the ethos of constructivism was the result. Lenin had coined the slogan 'electrification + soviets = socialism', and constructivism followed this concept: its aim was to reveal, not conceal. 'Work, organization, clarity', as Aleksei Gan put it in the first constructivist manifesto, of 1922. This was the year that Liubov Popova's mechanistic stage setting for *The magnanimous cuckold* was seen at the Meyerhold Theatre in Moscow. The year before, she and Aleksandr Vesnin had produced designs for a mass festival on Khodinskoe field: *Struggle and victory*. Cables from two airships carrying revolutionary slogans linked two constructivist stage sets: *The fortress of capital* and *The city of the future*, the latter dynamic and mechanistic. The spectacle, to be directed by Meyerhold, would have used massive resources. The new state, swept by famine and still under Allied blockade, was forced to cancel it.

The 'Factory of the Eccentric Actor' or FEKS group proclaimed Charlie Chaplin as hero, and the rhythm of American machinery as the model. The Blue Blouse agit-prop theatre groups – over four hundred strong by the late 1920s – formed 'living newspapers' or human tableaux, with titles such as 'Us and Henry Ford' or 'Propellor'. Vladimir Pashkov's design for the Lenin Library looks at first sight like a giant boiler.

'In this terrifying world made of frost, stale herrings, rags, typhoid fever, arrests, bread lines and armed soldiers, one first night followed the other, and every evening theatres were jammed. Towards the middle of a show the huge unheated houses were warmed up by the breath of the audience. Lights would flicker and often go out, there was little current and no coal ... in operas, members of orchestras played with their fur coats on and fur caps over their ears, and steam came from brass instruments as if they were locomotive pipes or smokestacks.' (Viktor Shklovsky)

→
The 1934 airship fund stamp, one of a set of five, shows the gondolas of Airship Lenin over Moscow and the 1926 radio mast by Shukov, an early constructivist icon

In the aftermath of the famine years, and under Lenin's New Economic Policy (NEP) of 1921, which allowed a degree of private enterprise as a pragmatic response to appalling shortages, Tatlin turned his attention to more immediate realities. Under the slogan 'not the old, not the new, but the necessary', he designed economic stoves with built-in airing cupboards and ovens, and an overcoat with different detachable linings for the Leningradodezhda firm. There was also a notable bentwood chair. Theatre design and book illustration followed, while preparatory work began on a novel man-powered glider: the 'Letatlin' or flying bicycle. The initial research for this project was carried out under the auspices of the Commissariat of Enlightenment's Experimental Laboratory for Material Culture, which Tatlin headed. Appropriately, the Laboratory was situated in the belfry of the Novodevichii convent. In 1930, after Mayakovsky's suicide, he and his students designed and constructed the bier that took the poet's body to the cemetry of this convent.

Tatlin, the sailor who wanted to fly, never achieved his dream, one as old as time, famously explored by that earlier genius Leonardo da Vinci. In spite of the support and collaboration of the famed aviator K. Artseuler, who had been a brigade commander in the Red Army, and was also an artist, a ten metre hop proved the limit.

Tatlin returned to the theme of ornithopters, participating in a conference on 'non-rigid wing flight' at the Zhukovsky Air Academy in January 1953, shortly before his death in March of that year. Stalin died in that month too. By this time, however, the prime area of aeronautic research and development focussed on rocket propulsion, and just four years later, the Soviet conquest of space began with the first successful satellite: Sputnik.

Sputnik anniversary cover and matching postmark

Paradoxically, on the stamps of the period, more constructivist inspired designs, incorporating the iconographic airships and industrial features, appeared alongside the traditionalist portraits. The extraordinary 1930 issue, ostensibly commemorating the Graf Zeppelin flight to Moscow, is in fact a small poster exhorting the first five year plan to be completed in four; the original design is by V. Kostyanitsyn

Heroes of labour

Vladimir Tatlin's model tower of 1919 had been constructed from scraps of timber, its spiral form expressing, according to the Soviet critic Pounin, humanity's dynamic climb to liberation. But with the five year plans and the onset of forced industrialization, the dreams of such projects were set aside for a crude utilitarianism. The horrors of the first industrial revolution, documented by Friedrich Engels and Victorian factory inspectors, were now condensed into a single short epoch. American technicians and European socialist architects helped to ameliorate such major projects as the new city of Magnitogorsk: Ernst May, from the relative comfort of Moscow, Mart Stam and Hannes Meyer on site in Siberia. Max Alpert's photograph of the young worker arriving there captures the pathos of these poorly equipped heroes of labour. The attempt to build the first projects with such inchoate labour and materials often resulted in technical failure: helping to discredit the architects of a modernism that may now seem premature, heroic.

The lines of verse are extracted from Mayakovsky's 'Story of Khrenov about Kuznetskstroy and the people of Kuznetsk': a massive iron and steel town in Siberia.

Workers
    sit there
        in the fug
and munch
    their soggy bread.
Louder than hunger
    whispers beat
and drown
    the rain-drops
        drear:
'In four years' time
    there'll be
a garden-city
    here!
And bands of bears
    sent flying,
        where
explosions
    crack
    and boom.
A hundred-pithead giant
    here
will burrow
    earth's
    dark womb.
Here
    rows of factories
    we'll raise,
through sirens
    steam
    will run.
Siberia
    we will set ablaze
with Martins'*
    hundred suns.

↗
The 1934 anti-war stamps, including the 5k 'Clouds of war', follow, in simplified form, Rodchenko's 1930 montage 'The war of the future'

*Martins was a brand of steel furnace

Volga famine relief
issue: one of a set
from 1921

→
The early stamps of
1918–22 reflected the
dire situation: savings
stamps authorized
for postal use, mas-
sive inflation and over-
printing, and crude
famine relief issues.
In marked contrast to
these was the radical
typography and bold
photomontage of
LEF. But by 1922, the
working class made
its appearance on the
definitive issues

Lenin and *LEF*

The spectre that had been haunting Europe since 1848 finally materialized through Lenin's revolutionary dialectic. Seizing power in Petrograd had proved easy enough, holding onto it proved far more taxing. In the first elections to the new constituent assembly, the Socialist-Revolutionaries from the countryside won 410 out of 707 seats, the Bolsheviks from the cities a mere 175. A coalition agreement between them allowed the revolution to con-tinue, until the treaty of Brest-Litovsk in March. Lenin had promised peace, but the massive territory ceded to the Germans alienated the left Social-Revolutionaries, who withdrew from the coalition and resorted to first assassinating the German ambas-sador, then staging an armed uprising after shooting a leading Bolshevik in Petrograd. Lenin himself was shot and wounded by one of the Social-Revolutionaries, Fanya Kaplan, in Moscow. This wounding proved to be a decisive contributing factor in Lenin's subsequent, ultimately fatal strokes. These events in particular, against a background of continuing civil war, became the justification for the 'Red terror' of autumn 1918, signalled by the execution of the tsar's family. The constituent assembly was dissolved, and the first step towards a single party state, maintained by counter-intelligence – the Cheka – was established.

Politically, then, there was the strictest discipline; in striking contrast to relative freedom in non-political areas – in particular, the arts. The antics of the frustrated futurists before 1917, in the city café society, may have irritated the sober revolutionaries, but the way they rallied to the new regime allowed them free reign in what became known as the 'left dictatorship of the arts' under Lenin's cultural commissar Anatoly Lunacharsky. The board of the new state department of art, IZO, included Altman, Kandinsky, Rodchenko and Shterenberg. The futurist poet Vladimir Mayakovsky was the editor of the magazine *LEF*, the Left Front of the Arts. New free studios were set up in place of the old academies. Agit-prop trains and river steamers spread the message through the countryside as the civil war con-tinued. What the peasants made of

this, 70 per cent of them still illiterate, was insignificant, set against their new-found ownership of the land they worked. Their support was the decisive factor in defeating the White armies of the hated old regime. The massively attended funeral of the old anarchist Kropotkin, in 1921, after the conclusion of the civil war and the end of the allied blockade, recognized this common aim. But by this time, Lenin was looking for help in the 'battle against futurism': 'Is it not possible to discover somewhere reliable anti-futurists?'

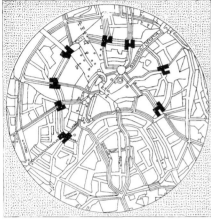

El Lissitzky's sky-hooks were planned to form a ring of inhabited triumphal gateways, focussing on the Kremlin: functional monumentalism

Siren song

'We shall scrape the sky with concrete' wrote Mayakovsky in the first flush of post-revolutionary excitement. Vladimir Krinsky attempted designs for a 'Bolshevik' skyscraper; Lissitzky – the cantilevered sky-hooks of 1924, which would focus on the Kremlin from the outer ring road. Cantilevers were predominant in the ateliers of Ladovsky and Krinsky, in the new free design studios of Vkhutemas. A symphony of factory sirens was the prelude to massive industrialization: the first five year plan. The USA was the model for the new USSR. (Edgar Varese's *Ionization* of 1931 captured the rhythms of New York, but with a police siren.) Translations of Henry Ford's works sold like hot cakes; where earlier Germany had been the model to emulate, the focus now shifted to New York and Chicago, especially after Mayakovsky's tour of the USA. Krinsky's project takes the well-known 'Chicago frame' as the starting point for more expressive tectonics indicating the different internal spatial organization: a device that Le Corbusier would later use in his Algiers skyscraper project.

In Lenin's *Immediate tasks of the Soviet government*, the new order is based on F.W. Taylor's 'scientific management' principles:

'The Soviet republic must at all costs adopt all that is valuable in the achievements of science and technology in this field. The possibility of building socialism depends exactly upon our success in combining the Soviet power and the Soviet organization of administration with the up-to-date achievements of capitalism.'

Marxism may have come from Germany, together with the Zeppelin, and German and Dutch architects to plan the new settlements, but it was American engineers and technicians who built the factories. Albert Kahn Associates carried out some 500 projects. The massive steel works of Magnitogorsk, powered by the Dnieprestroi Dam, engraved by Troitsky in the air express stamps of 1932, was based on Pittsburg. The American engineers lived in a separate, American-styled suburb. The foreign architects who came, such as Ernst May, Hannes Mayer, J.B. van Loghem, and Mart Stam, were accorded small privileges also.

Under Stalin's iron rule, however, Lenin's up-to-dateness was abandoned in favour of the more archaic method: slave labour. The number of apparently arbitrary arrests and deportations to the labour camps – some five million people in all – bore a direct relationship to the demands of rapid industrial growth. Women were not exempt. 'Blatnoi' or super-hooligans controlled the huts. Those who had not died would be released by Krushchev in the mid-1950s. In the most intense period, after the loss of some 20 million citizens in the Second World War, the few Soviet women who dared to marry Allied servicemen received sentences of between 10 and 25 years. Communists from Europe, who had come to help build socialism, found themselves transported also, as a result of Stalin's paranoia and chauvinism. The revolutionary Bolsheviks had tried to fight such nationalism, which, in Germany too – even with its huge socialist, later communist party – allowed Hitler and the fascists into power. So to be 'cosmopolitan' was a crime in both the Reich and the USSR. Yet the constructivist spirit survived throughout Europe in those dark days.

1923 saw the first definitive stamp issues with the new currency values, worth one million paper roubles: the weather-beaten features of the peasant now joined the prototype soldier and worker. The first airmails followed in 1924, and had to be surcharged even before they were issued

At the end of 1922, a competition for a Palace of Labour was announced, to mark the the new Soviet state, now formally recognized after the Rapallo Treaty. The programme called for a combination of public and party functions: house of the Soviets, congress hall, theatre, Ministry of Culture, committee rooms, museum and restaurant. The brief for this new building type went on to state:

'The multiple aspects of the Palace of Labour should be reflected both internally and externally and should be expressed in simple, contemporary forms, without reference to any specific style of any past era whatsoever.'

The Vesnin brothers' solution, with its clearly articulated forms dynamically interlocked, exposed concrete frame, and flurry of technological elements – radio masts, pylons, news screen, nautical ventilators – was hailed as the first major constructivist work. The scheme was widely published, and praised. Le Corbusier sent a signed photograph to the 'founders of constructivism'. What should have been the birth of a radical new style to match the new state proved a turning point in the opposite direction, as the prize was awarded to N.A. Trotsky's clumsily monumental design – the jury was nominated by fellow academic Zholtovsky. This would be a prelude to the later, more notorious, Palace of the Soviets competition. This first symbolic project to celebrate Labour (rather than Soviets) was quickly abandoned, and the two-faced Moscow Hotel built in its place.

In 1924 the incapacitated Lenin finally died, and the campaign against Leon Trotsky, creator of the Red Army, began in earnest. It was orchestrated by Stalin, already General Secretary of the new USSR: a seemingly dull administrative post for which there had been no competition; Lenin's early warning against him in 1922 having been forgotten.

By the time – 1927 – of El Lissitzky's cover design for works from the architecture faculty at the Vkhutemas, a brilliant student had emerged from Vesnin's studio: Ivan Leonidov. His diploma project for the Lenin Library took the constructivist idea to its refined conclusion: the carefully composed drawings that seemed to derive from Lissitzky's 'proun' paintings, the pure prismatic forms of the highly crafted model (a light bulb used for the globe auditorium), and mechanistic armatures. But with the deportation of Trotsky to Alma Ata in this same year, the tide was rapidly turning against any form of intellectual experiment or opposition to centralized directives. The Lenin Library competition was won by a neo-classical solution: exactly the sort of architecture that became the hallmark of authoritarian regimes the world over.

On the site of the proposed Palace of Labour now stands the Moscow Hotel. There is an apocryphal story that has Stalin approving the drawings of the hotel, which showed alternative treatments for the symmetrical wings, drawn like this for comparison and to save time. The architect, A.V. Shchusev, had been given the job of redesigning a constructivist scheme by two young architects, which by then would not have got through. Shchusev did not dare to speak up, and the design was built exactly as drawn. A further irony was that the image featured on the label of a well-known vodka brand

МОСКВА
1927

АРХИТЕКТУРА

АРХИТЕКТУРА

ВХУТЕМАС

ИВАН ЛЕОНИДОВ

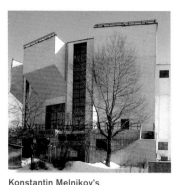

Konstantin Melnikov's
Rusakov club, Moscow
(1928–9).
Photographed in 1974

Details of Georgy
Krutikov's 'flying city'
project (1928)

The faculty of architecture within the Vkhutemas was formed in 1920, against a background of universal labour service, imminent famine, and the creation of a single-party state. The extraordinary and innovative work produced in these studios in the 1920s looked forward to better things. Inspirational teachers – Ginzburg, Golossov, Ladovsky, Krinsky, Melnikov ('just up from our school desks, we became professors') – worked alongside the older academics, such as Shchusev and Zholtovsky. One student in particular, from Aleksandr Vesnin's studio, would acquire legendary status: Ivan Leonidov. His diploma project for the Lenin Library (a competition that his tutor was also entering) would soon become the focus for widespread disapproval of all radical modernism. The break with the past expressed in the pure, undecorated forms, the open spatiality and technocratic emphasis were like a red rag to the vulgar Marxists who came to the fore in the 1930s. 'Leonidovshchina' became an 'ism' alongside 'Trotskyism'. Half a century later these same features would come under attack from influential academics in the capitalist world: once again in the name of the common people; but this time, technology had made such architecture realizable.

Leonidov's response to such criticism, as represented in his 1934 entry for the Narkomtiazhprom (Commissariat for Heavy Industry) in Red Square, seemed to contain a degree of irony. The massive towers dwarf St Basil's Cathedral, their forms more elaborated than the minimalist tower of the Lenin Library, their grouping more picturesque. A giant polychromatic drum marks the workers' club contained within a colonnade of tapered columns: this the compositional balance to the existing cathedral. The conical drum emerging through a grid of columns suggests a precedent for Le Corbusier's assembly hall in Chandigarh; while Le Corbusier limited the decoration to the inside, Leonidov wanted it outside. The cylindrical tower of glazed brick interspersed with vertical slots of clear glass, and with its projecting curved balconies like some constructivist fungi, would have taken Bruno Taut's glass architecture to undreamt of

heights. Leonidov died in 1959, his only built work a highly formalist set of stairs in the garden of the Narkomtiazhprom Sanatorium, in which he did manage to include both a projecting balcony and the tapered columns from this project.

If Tatlin's tower was the earliest symbol of the revolution, Leonidov's work, up until 1930, represented the distillation of the liberating potential of the constructivist ethos. His concept of space was ineffable. The Palace of Culture project for 1930, published in *Contemporary Architecture*, broke from the already traditional form of workers' clubs, so expressively shaped by Konstantin Melnikov in particular, to propose instead an area of activities, pavilions and communications within an open landscaped grid: in deliberate contrast to the dense urban space surrounding. It is the genesis of what would become, in a distorted form, the consumerist theme park. Extensive glazed surfaces would maximize contact with the landscape and sky: hardly practical, considering the Moscow climate. But a version of the proposed glass pyramid sports hall would be built in Milton Keynes some 50 years later.

The conquest of space and romance of flight were predominant themes in Leonidov's work: the first project for the Lenin Library even included an aerotram cable link into the heart of Moscow, from its site on the surrounding hills. Against a background of economic crisis, massive deportation and the purge trials that accompanied massive industrial growth, another remarkable student, Georgy Krutikov, worked out details for a flying city, in Ladovsky's studio.

↗
Constructivist dreams would be partly realized with the first satellite launch – Sputnik – in 1957, and more remarkably with the first manned space flight, by Yuri Gargarin, in 1961: celebrated by a set of three stamps including the 'se-tenant' label featuring part of Nikita Krushchev's speech. No supporter of modern art, for all his denouncing the cult of Stalin, Krushchev suggested in one of his more restrained outbursts that such artists 'should have their trousers removed and be sat in a bed of nettles'

са 5 ОВРЕМЕННАЯ РХИТЕНТУРА 1930

ДВОРЕЦ КУЛЬТУРЫ
И. ЛЕОНИДОВ

Early martyrs of the space race commemorated in 1934; here showing Fedoseyenko the captain

On the road to the futurist city

El Lissitzky was raised in the unique Jewish community of Vitebsk, immortalized by his fellow artist Chagall. In 1909 he moved to Darmstadt, to study at what was then the most progressive architectural polytechnic. Travelling through Europe, the 1914 war forced his return to Russia. This background, together with his great talent, marked him out for the role of cultural-ambassador/designer for the new Soviet government of the 1920s. His paintings and reliefs – the 'prouns', a fusion of painting and architecture – had already become well-known, particularly to Van Doesburg and the Stijl group in Holland. The 1919 street poster *Beat the Whites with the Red wedge* was a brilliant marriage of abstraction and propaganda. The first major exhibition of the new Soviet arts opened in 1922 in Berlin, with Lissitzky lecturing.

Invited to show his work at the Kestner Gesellschaft in Hanover, he met Sophie Küppers, the widow of the society's artistic director, and subsequently took her and her two sons to Moscow, and married her.

El Lissitzky and his wife Sophie, together with his brother and the revolutionary film director Dziga Vertov – 'the man with the movie camera' – on the yellow brick road to the city of the future, where Chernikhov's architectural fantasies might meet with Leonidov's projects: the sky crisscrossed with airships, the stratosphere reached by balloon, the subterranean tunnelled for the Moscow Metro.

There is a haunting moment in Andrei Tarkovsky's autobiographical film masterpiece *Mirror*, showing the launch of such a balloon, seemingly in slow motion. It surely refers to this tragedy, just as other newsreel elements within the film refer to similar disasters. Even in his earlier film *Andrei Roublev*, set in the Middle Ages, there was, in the script, an episode that would show a peasant's fatal attempt to fly with homemade wings from a cathedral belfry. Tarkovsky described in his book *Sculpting in time* how they decided to substitute a clumsy rag and leather balloon: a more subtle image, but possibly still an ironic reminder of Tatlin in the bell tower of the Novodevichii convent.

Of all the new Soviet designers, El Lissitzky was the most influential and international. In the 1920s, as exhibition designer for the new state, he travelled throughout Europe, spreading hope for radically minded artists, especially in Holland and Germany. His new approach to typography converted Piet Zwart, persuading him to leave architecture to become a 'typotect'. But while Zwart was to have some influence on Dutch postal design, in the USSR more traditional illustrators held sway in this field – in striking contrast to Soviet films, books and posters. For example, the first issues of *LEF*, designed by Rodchenko, used photomontage and overprinting on a classic model of constructionist typography.

↗
The beautifully coloured vertical format 1933 issue formed one of a set, designed by Zavialov, to commemorate the altitude record set that September by Prokofiev, Godunov and Bernbaum, in the balloon 'Stratosat USSR'. They reached 58,700 feet. Just two months later, the USA reached 61,000 feet in the balloon 'A Century of Progress', with Settle and Fordney. This pushed the Russians to try again, and in January 1934 they reached 72,000 feet, before the gondola cable broke, plummeting it to earth and killing the crew: Fedoseyenko, Vasenko and Vsyskin, who were honoured with a set of stamps in 1934. This was one of the first sacrifices in what would become the USSR/USA space race. A similar accident befell the Americans, but they managed to parachute to safety. In 1935 the USA set a new record of 72,000 feet in 'Explorer 2', with Anderson and Stevens

El Lissitzky, *Beat the Whites with the Red wedge*, poster (1919)

Le Corbusier's
Centrosoyuz building,
Moscow (1929–36).
Photographed in 1974

Imagine Le Corbusier's surprise when he visited the set of Sergei Eisenstein's *The old and the new* and found a clone of his architecture, mocked up in the woods outside Moscow. The set designer was the architect Andrei Burov, seen here with Eisenstein and Le Corbusier, and looking a little too affectedly like a twin. Le Corbusier was in Moscow to defend his entry for the Centrosoyuz competition, for which he had been invited to enter by Nikolai Popov, director of the Centrosoyuz Paris office. Coming after his humilation in the League of Nations competition, the invitation seemed an indication of the new Soviet state's support for progressive architecture, and would offer the promise of his first major public building, alongside the Salvation Army hostel in Paris: both sharing a strong social programme.

The old and the new, a propaganda film in support of Stalin's collectivization programme, tells the story of a peasant woman's struggle to establish a co-operative against local resistance, with a bull and tractor as the key elements. A strange poster shows the bull driving the tractor. The striking white modern style of the envisioned utopian collective dairy was deliberately propagandist; there too were the admired grain silos. But Stalin was not happy, and insisted on changing the ending. Far worse was to come, with the disastrous collectivization of agriculture, which brought about another famine in 1932. This brutal reversal of Lenin's original New Economic Policy was typical of Stalin's twists and turns, which found a parallel in Andrei Burov's architectural career. Unlike Le Corbusier, who had started with the past and moved towards the future, Burov started with the future – purism and then constructivism – before moving to the past. By the 1930s, of course, this was mandatory in Stalinist Russia. While Lenin held conservative views on culture, he insisted that this was a field that should include everyone, not just an élite. Stalin and the populist factions would use this broad concept to create a cultural monolith: 'socialist realism'. The better architects, most noticeably the Vesnin brothers, would struggle to accomodate this demand: 'the people have a right to colonnades'. While Lenin had been used to delegate – after all, the radical Lunacharsky had been his Minister of Culture – Stalin would oversee all aspects of life.

Andrei Burov: from the
new to the old; the first
postmodernist?

Ilya Golossov's
Zuyev club, Moscow
(1926–8).
Photographed in 1974

The decision in 1928 to award Le Corbusier the commission for the Centrosoyuz headquarters, after a staged competition entered by the Vesnin brothers, Ginzburg and Leonidov, as well as Peter Behrens and Max Taut from Germany, represented a foothold for the new architecture in the first socialist republic. Le Corbusier's scheme was featured on the cover of the magazine *The Construction of Moscow*, designed by the constructivists Vasily Elkin and Gustav Klutsis; and in a gesture of magnanimity, his fellow competitors Ginzburg and the Vesnins, of the OSA group, weighed in on his side.

The 1920s had already seen an unprecedented series of projects reflecting the new social structure: palaces of culture, communal housing, and the workers' clubs. Ilya Golossov's Zuyev club, on the corner of Lesny Street in Moscow, completed in 1928, being one of the most influential. Construction of the Centrosoyuz started on site in 1930, with Nikolai Kolli as site architect. In 1918 Kolli had produced one of the best-known pieces of propaganda art: the Red Wedge monument in Voskresenskaya Square, a sculptural version of Lissitzky's poster *Beat the Whites with the Red wedge*. When work on the Centrosoyuz was suspended as a result of all resources being directed to the industrial priorities of the first five year plan in 1931, Kolli went to work with the Vesnin brothers on the design of Dniepr dam. By 1932, Lissitzky is seen photographing the completed dam structure, while Le Corbusier's style comes in for tough criticism from this socialist ambassador of construc-

tivism. Aleksandr Vesnin loyally insists that the Centrosoyuz is simply the best building in Moscow for a hundred years. By the time of its completion in 1936, however, the original clients had disappeared in the nightmarish flux of the five year plans – the state replacing the co-ops of the first NEP – and the tide of opinion had turned against modern architecture with the decisive centralization of the profession in 1932. This coincided with the Palace of the Soviets competition result: a victory for the traditionalist camp.

Le Corbusier's constructivist entry was unplaced. The site – unlike that of the 1923 Palace of Labour competition – already had a building on it: Konstantin Ton's Church of Christ the Saviour, built in 1832. In 1931 this was demolished and foundations for Boris Iofan's winning scheme were opened up. The original tripartite solution was now scooped up into a monstrous monolith capped by a gigantic figure of Lenin (minus his cap) in an edifice that owed much to Cecil B. De Mille: the first postmodernist Babylon.

Le Corbusier at least managed to get the final payment of his Centrosoyuz fees in 1939, just before the Nazi/Soviet pact was signed: another piece of paper that Hitler would tear up. During the war, the Palace foundations filled with water. Subsequently, in a stroke of inspired pragmatism, they were turned into a grand heated swimming pool: one of Moscow's popular meeting places.

In the 1990s, after the sudden collapse of the USSR and despite economic chaos, the original cathedral has been rebuilt in steel and concrete. History running backwards.

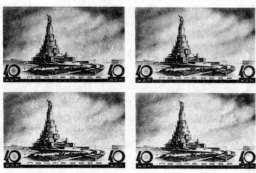

ПЕРВЫЙ ВСЕСОЮЗНЫЙ
СЪЕЗД АРХИТЕКТОРОВ

МОСКВА-1937

A commemorative block of four stamps – issued in 1937 to mark the first international congress of architects in Moscow – illustrated the final design for the Palace of the Soviets

↗
By 1960, a somewhat idealized portrait of an architect appears on the definitive issues that had originally featured just workers, peasants, and soldiers

→
Looked at with hindsight, Le Corbusier's entry seems to fit in perfectly with the spirit of the time, reflected in the 1931 airship construction fund stamps

Ginzburg and the green city

Moisei Ginzburg's communnal housing on Novinsky Avenue, Moscow (1928–9). Photographed in 1974

If the Vesnin brothers were the founders of constructivism in architecture, El Lissitzky the ambassador, and Leonidov the visionary, Moisei Ginzburg was the practising theoretician. His *Style and epoch*, written at the same time as Le Corbusier's *Vers une architecture* and published in 1924, with the jacket a collage designed by Aleksandr Vesnin, remains the key work from the period. Like Le Corbusier, he attempted a synthesis of classicism and the machine: aircraft, ships and grain silos are used to illustrate a similar thesis. But unlike Le Corbusier, he includes projects by other architects in the closing chapter, including Melnikov, Lavinsky, Gan, Golossov and the Vesnins. Together with the Vesnins, Ginzburg founded the most significant constructivist group, OSA, with its own architectural review *Contemporary Architecture*, which ran from 1926 to 1930. The first issue opened with Aleksei Gan's bold typography proclaiming: 'Contemporary architecture must crystallize the new socialist way of life'.

Ginzburg's was an exceptional talent, and the experimental housing block on Novinsky Avenue, Moscow, built in 1928–9 could be seen as the first major demonstration of Le Corbusier's 'five points of a new architecture' and a precursor to the first Unité d'Habitation at Marseilles: but where that would stand self-contained like an ocean liner in a sea of green, Ginzburg's concept tied the linear block with enclosed corridors to a group of communal and service buildings. In the event, only one of these was built, and was taken over by the Party as a printing shop. Due to the acute shortage of living space in the city, extra families were billeted into the double-height apartments with their minimal kitchens, and the experiment was deemed a failure.

This experience prompted a dramatic change in Ginzburg's attitude to housing, first demonstrated in a competition for a 'green city' for workers to enjoy the equivalent of the weekend dacha. With the massive pressure of the rapid industrialization, even the party leaders conceded the need for amelioration. Ginzburg and Mikhail Barshch proposed a ribbon of cabins, standing on 'pilotis', threaded across the countryside with an east-west orientation. Everyone would enjoy an uninterrupted view of sunrise and set. These would be linked at key points to communal blocks; and the assumption was that everyone had a car. Some hope! Nevertheless a prototype was built using prefabricated components, and the idea was later developed in the form of freestanding family units. This was surely one of the most poetic projects of the time: a communitarian Walden. In 1934 the Swiss-born Albert Frey, who had worked with Le Corbusier, together with Lawrence Kocher of New York, built an American version of this on Long Island: the opening project in Alfred Roth's *The new architecture*.

The first set of stamps
to commemorate
Mayakovsky's death
were issued in 1940,
followed by a fiftieth
birthday anniversary
set in 1943

Sky skaters

In 1927 the foremost poet of the revolution, Vladimir Mayakovsky, wrote
'October poem' to celebrate its tenth
anniversary. These lines come from the
poem's final section. His revolutionary
futurism had been like a beacon in
the darkening days. Mayakovsky's
death in 1930 – by his own hand –
seemed to mark the end of simple
optimism. His funeral bier, designed
by Tatlin, was followed by thousands,
in the largest procession since that
for Kropotkin. While Lenin hated this
work, Stalin greatly admired it and
insisted on honouring his memory:
an indication that there was 'a spark
in that black heart', as someone dared
to remark – the pianist whose recorded
performance from Moscow radio was
playing when Stalin died.

The sky
     high above me
silky-blue.
Life
    was really
never
    so good!
Sky-skaters
       whizz-by
aviators.
Those aviators
      belong to me.
Like a towering tree
     I rose.
Into the middle of next week
they'll knock
    my foes.

'Red Army Star
Caramels' toffee
wrapper, by
Mayakovsky and
Rodchenko, in revol-
utionary populist style

Konstantin Melnikov's
Makhorka pavilion
(for the state tobacco
company), at the All-
Russian Agricultural
Exhibition, Moscow,
1923

1923 had seen the first All-Russian Agricultural Exhibition, planned by I.V. Zholtovsky, who also designed the main pavilion. This was the most complete realization to date of Lenin's call for 'monumental propaganda', and formed a showpiece for the New Economic Policy. This was the policy that reintroduced private enterprise, even encouraging the peasant/farmers to 'enrich yourselves'. With the introduction of the NEP in 1921, the short-lived 'left dictatorship of the arts' had come to an end. As market forces replaced state support, the nouveau riche, who were the natural product of this policy, did not patronize the experimental. It was at this point that the most politically motivated artists turned to product design and typography. But in the field of architecture, there was dramatic innovation. Konstantin Melnikov's Makhorka pavilion, with its dramatic geometry and expressive structure, was the forerunner of the striking pavilion at the 1925 Paris Exposition des Arts Décoratifs, which gained him international recognition. Aleksandra Ekster and Feodor Gladkov produced the constructivist Isvestya pavilion, which took the form of a tower, and Ludwig designed a daring suspension structure for the concert area.

The Ford motor company, which had started trading already in 1919, flourished in this period. Between 1922 and 1925 they increased sales from 600 to 11,000. The first agricultural revolution was driven with Fordson tractors, made initially in the Pulitov factory: one of the original Bolshevik strongholds.

Clouds were already gathering as Lenin lay dying. His policy was overturned with the first five year plan, which brought the collectivization of agriculture and the elimination of those very peasants who previously had been encouraged to enrich themselves. Stalin is here admiring the first diesel tractor from the Cheliabinsk factory: one of more than 500 projects carried out by the American firm of Albert Kahn Associates. With the Wall Street stock market crash of 1929 and the ensuing depression, these vast contracts must have seemed something of a godsend, even if they were in the godless Soviet Union. The USA

had opened up trade in 1928, via the AMTORG Trading Co. But by 1932 this firm had pulled out, as a result of domestic pressure. Though, oddly, the USA finally recognized the USSR in 1933.

By the 1930s, the original constructivist theatre and Laboratory of Dance had ossified as state spectacle. Individuals became, all too clearly, cogs in the monolithic machine: in ironic parallel with the emerging empire of Hollywood.

The new factories, which the Americans initially feared might be used to produce armaments, were to do just that – but for use against the Nazis, and with US support. The decisive tank battle at Kursk in 1943 was the beginning of the end for the Third Reich. In the muddy terrain, the Soviet machines proved more manoeuvrable than the heavier German models, which had the added weakness of merely frontal armouring.

The T34 tanks – mass produced at an incredible rate in the factories that had been moved beyond Nazi reach, to 'Tankograd' on the other side of the Urals – proved one of the decisive weapons of the war. At half the weight of the 55 ton German giant 'Tiger' tanks, and with a 76 mm gun, radically sloped armour, extra wide tracks and faster speed, the T34 was a masterpiece of functional design.

Three continents: Le Corbusier's utopianism

If it yearns after primordial truths,
the spirit destroys itself;
if it weds the earth it thrives.
   Max Jacob:
   Philosophies, no. 1, 1924

The Ozenfant studio,
Paris (1923–4)

The extraordinary compilation of old and new, sacred and industrial, massive and lightweight, that Le Corbusier attempted to synthesize in *Vers une architecture*, with its novel juxtaposition of the Parthenon and a Delago coupé, included a chapter on mass-production of houses. This presented a set of designs by Le Corbusier and Pierre Jeanneret, his cousin and partner, concluding with a photograph of the recently completed studio for Ozenfant, whose name did not appear.

These designs in reinforced concrete included the three basic house forms that would appear in all the later projects: the maison 'Dom-Ino' with its concrete frame; the 'Citrohan', having a double-height living space overlooked by a gallery level, with load-bearing cross walls; and 'Monol', with a barrel-vaulted roof exposed internally. The urban prototype was a perimeter block of 'freehold maisonettes' with hanging gardens; four double-height storeys high plus a penthouse level. A prototype unit would be built for the 1925 Paris Exposition des Arts Décoratifs, but the composite idea was sadly never taken up.

The Ozenfant studio had little to do with mass production: the industrial-style metal windows were specially made. But on a potentially awkward corner site, the composition is masterly. The placing of the major space on the top level, to take max-

imum advantage of light and view, studio-style, would be a feature of later houses.

By 1925, however, Le Corbusier's partnership with Ozenfant had broken up and the magazine *L'Esprit Nouveau*, started in 1920, that he had edited with Ozenfant and Dermée, and which had been the first outlet for the ideas in *Vers une architecture*, had ceased publication after 28 issues. He and Ozenfant had done rather well in purchasing modern art on commission for the banker Raoul La Roche, and in then persuading him to build a little house and gallery adjoining a house for Pierre Jeanneret. In this unique double house, now the offices of the Le Corbusier Foundation, the major space was a triple-height hallway, linking the domestic and gallery spaces with a first-floor 'passarelle'. This arrangement provided the grandest entrance elevation of all the Corbusian villas. Other studies were completed for Lipchitz and Miestchaninoff, at the same time as the first workers' housing for the factory owner and art patron Henry Frugès. Charles-Edouard Jeanneret, now known as Le Corbusier, from the small town of La Chaux-de-Fonds in Switzerland, had established himself at the centre of the art world in Paris.

Espirit Nouveau
pavilion

'A great epoch has begun; there exists a new spirit': Le Corbusier, *Vers une architecture*, 1923

A classical 'déjeuner sur l'herbe' with wife Yvonne

My Egypt was the title of a painting by the American artist Charles Demuth. It simply portrayed the gigantic twin towers of a grain silo, in a style close to the 'Neue Sachlichkeit' school of Europe in the 1920s. Demuth, together with Charles Sheeler and Joseph Stella, celebrated the new, for them heroic, landscape of industrial America. Early Egypt had been the granary of the Roman Empire, which had helped to spread the desert by exhaustive cultivation; but just as there is Memphis, Tennessee, there surely was an Egypt, Iowa, or somewhere on the great plains to which Demuth's title refers.

For Le Corbusier, in his seminal *Vers une architecture*, Greece or Rome was the architecture of prisms, cubes and cylinders, pyramids or spheres; and the cut-away axonometric of the Temple at Thebes is used to demonstrate the thesis of the plan as generator. Such examples as the pyramids and the temple of Luxor were cited in the first of the book's 'Three reminders to architects', titled 'Mass', which opened with a photograph of a twin-stack Baltimore grain silo; in fact the nine illustrations for this chapter were all of grain stores.

Walter Gropius had been one of the first young European architects to draw attention to American industrial buildings, with an article published in the *Deutscher Werkbund Jahrbuch* of 1913. Le Corbusier, who had met Gropius earlier, while briefly working in Behrens's studio in Berlin, alongside Mies van der Rohe, used many of the same photographs for his text; though his collaborator, Amédée Ozenfant, wrote in his diary that he painted out the Greek-style pediments. So the quaintly topped silos of Buenos Aires, featured by Gropius in 1913, appeared in *Vers une architecture* in 1923, in purer form and assigned to Canada.

The chapter on 'Mass' closed like this, with capital letters for emphasis: 'Thus we have the American grain elevators and factories, the magnificent FIRST-FRUITS of the new age. THE AMERICAN ENGINEERS OVERWHELM WITH THEIR CALCULATIONS OUR EXPIRING ARCHITECTURE.'

Subsequent chapters would admire liners, airplanes and automobiles.

The 1923 airmail was a particularly fine example of the 'stylized sobriety' that made Swiss stamps a measure by which others were judged. But with the advent of photogravure in the 1930s, the firm of Courvoiser, at La Chaux-de-Fonds, would come to prominence

P. W. M. Cairo. 14/12/17

Philae

No. 351 Ventro & Zachos, Cairo & Luxor

Le Corbusier's development as a leading figure in the modern movement confirms Nikolaus Pevsner's theory of its evolution out of the Arts & Crafts movement. But his early efforts in this style would not be included in the first volume of his completed works. It was however the Villa Schwob, designed in 1916, that marked the first major step in his architectural career. Interestingly enough, it was being built as he returned to Paris to work on his patented 'Dom-Ino' system for concrete-framed houses, which takes up the first section of the *Oeuvre complète* published by Girsberger in 1930. Behind the brick-clad façades and eclectic details, the double-height living space with upper gallery facing a full-height window onto the landscape made its first appearance. The overambitious Pierre Jeanneret seriously underestimated the costs, and this, together with his absence in Paris during construction, led to his first law suit. Visiting the completed house while the court case was in progress, he was quick to bemoan the client's taste in furniture and decor – as ruining his nice spaces. An all too common complaint.

Pierre Jeanneret's departure in October 1917 to set up in Paris, leaving his assistant Marcel Montandon in charge of the job, coincided with the revolution in Russia. The Schwob family were to lose their extensive investments there. The draconian tsarist empire, with its large resources and subjugated labour force, had made investment highly attractive – at first.

The twin curved forms of the Villa Schwob would, in the subsequent period, appear only within the confines of an orthogonal grid. The more sensuous figures safely contained within the rigid columnar domain – an aspect of the so-called 'free plan', one of the 'five points of a new architecture' – or the picture plane of the purist paintings.

The *Still life with stacked plates* of 1920, with its collection of feminine curves, bottles and pipes facing us, may be less overt than the drawings of the Algerian prostitutes by whom Le Corbusier was intrigued, but given the sexual symbolism of the clay pipe (already evident in the genre paintings of the seventeenth-century Dutch painter Jan Steen) it is surprising that this aspect has been ignored in discussions of purism. These stress rather the everyday nature of the objects: as if all Parisian tables were laid with guitars, clay pipes, laboratory glassware and buttock-shaped mouldings.

By 1922, with the adopted name of 'Le Corbusier', he had set up a studio and practice with cousin Pierre, had met Yvonne Gallis, a fashion model, whom he would marry in 1930, and had designed the first two houses in the new style: Villa Vaucresson and the Ozenfant studio. However, it was the Esprit Nouveau pavilion for the 1925 Paris Exposition des Arts Décoratifs, with its double-height living room and outdoor terrace, that caused the greatest stir. The pavilion itself was a model apartment of the 'freehold maisonette' type illustrated in *Vers une architecture*, and was furnished with Thonet chairs, built-in fittings and purist paintings, together with the simple glassware and crockery they portrayed. Alongside, two curved dioramas contained models for the Villa Contemporaine and the Voisin Plan for Paris. Nothing could have seemed further removed from his artistic spirit than these totalitarian plans, and the overt apeal to big business and automania: the architect as master of the environment.

In the brave new world of the Voisin Plan – named after the aircraft manufacturer – 'Cartesian' office skyscrapers dwarf the continuous housing blocks, their profile a facsimile of the paving pattern at Piazza San Marco, Venice

The twin curves of the Villa Schwob reappeared as the solarium walls crowning the Villa Savoye, and formed the setting for the gymnastic sequence of Pierre Chenal's film *Architecture d'aujourd'hui*, made shortly after its completion in 1929

Pneu Vélo

Le Corbusier hires an old biplane to show off his first model housing project, at Pessac, in the Gironde. The lady is obviously impressed, but the two other men are busy looking at the camera.

A factory owner in Lège, near the dockyards of Arcachon, gave Le Corbusier the chance to put the idea of mass-produced concrete houses into practice by commissioning ten prototypes for the workers at his packing-case factory. It was his son, Henry Frugès, who had originally been asked to do the job; but he had been so impressed by one of Le Corbusier's articles in *L'Esprit Nouveau* – the forerunner to the celebrated *Vers une architecture* polemic – that he invited him to participate. Having brought all the necessary cement-mixing equipment – including the guns for application, which were highly expensive – Henry Frugès took the bold step of inviting Le Corbusier to proceed on a larger scale, for some two hundred units to be sold, on a fine site surrounded with pine trees at Pessac. Le Corbusier and Jeanneret's ambitious first plan proposed a version of the stacked 'freehold maisonettes' illustrated in *Vers une architecture*, with the liberated ground space used for playing fields and allotments. The elder Frugès however, as developer, sensibly insisted on houses, and the final layout for the fifty-odd units that were built achieved a fine balance of unity and variety within a far more humanely scaled layout. Frugès had also pleaded in vain for some decorative features: the final compromise was a polychromatic colour scheme.

The project had met with local hostility and obstruction since its inception, particularly from the architects of the region. The municipality held

up the water supply for many years. Known locally as 'Frugès' sugar cubes' – his factory made packing crates for sugar – the houses stood empty from their official opening in June 1926 to 1930, by which time Henry Frugès' father had died and he faced financial ruin. He went to recuperate in Algeria, and central government, invoking the Loucheur Law, found tenants for the estate, albeit from the poorest layer of Bordeaux society. So the Pessac experiment quickly deteriorated into a problem council estate (a pattern that would be used to discredit a similar, Corbusian-inspired project in the London Borough of Camden). Later, after the war, more affluent occupants were quick to add their own decorative features, incorporating every style but purism. This prompted the famous remark by Le Corbusier that 'it is always life that is right and the architect who is wrong'. On the other hand, the extreme simplicity of the initial plans allowed for a great variety of adaptation, and the ingenious handed layout provided individual privacy.

At the time, the only enthusiastic response came from Dr P. Winter, who was a friend of Le Corbusier and a member of the 'Faisceau' group, which saw the scheme, with its use of standardized components and emphasis on health and hygiene, as a perfect model for the national building policy of the Fascist state. But shortly after, Nazi ideologues would attack the similar houses at the Weissenhof as examples of Bolshevism.

The story of Pessac became the subject of the first classic of architectural sociology, Philippe Boudon's *Lived-in architecture*, published in 1969, with an introduction by Henri Lefebvre.

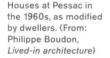

Houses at Pessac in the 1960s, as modified by dwellers. (From: Philippe Boudon, *Lived-in architecture*)

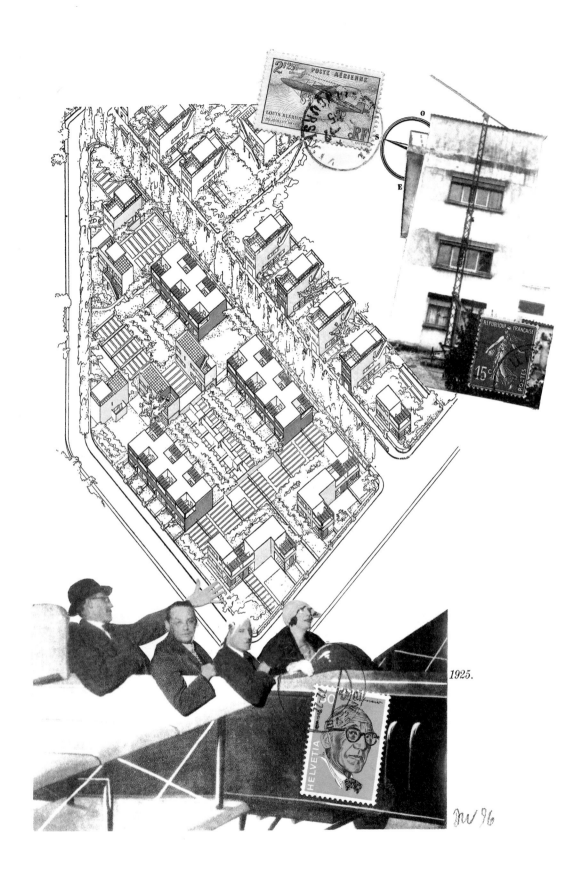

1925.

JW 96

The 1925 stamp designs marking the Paris Exposition des Arts Décoratifs, with their distinct emphasis on vases, suggest the impact that both Le Corbusier's and Melnikov's pavilions must have had in this decorative arts context

Marie Charlotte Amélie Jeanneret-Gris, a retired pianist and music teacher, sits at the table in the beautiful little house that her son designed for her on the edge of Lac Léman. Among the pots on the bookcase, a photograph of Charles-Edouard, who had adopted the title Le Corbusier from her ancestors the Le Corbésiers. This wonderfully convenient little bungalow had been designed at the same time as the big Paris exhibition of 1925, which had been celebrated with a multicoloured set of stamps. To think that Albert's little brother, who had started out engraving watches was now designing cities for three million people! And he hadn't spent a day in architectural school. But then, hadn't she always told him 'whatever you do, just do it'. And that brilliant artist Saul Steinberg had presented him with a diploma surely worth far more than a scrap of paper from the Beaux-Arts. It was a shame about that horrid carpet in the Esprit Nouveau pavilion though; it just didn't go with the first hi-tech staircase. And by the time the pavilion was finished, nearly three months after the opening, a lot of people must have missed it, and the most talked about was the Bolshevik pavilion by Konstantin Melnikov. Now there was a radical edge! Didn't it make the Esprit Nouveau look a bit too lavish by comparison?

When it came to persuading the big wigs to part with their money in the cause of Art, especially his, her boy did well. Hadn't poor Henry Frugès spent enough on Pessac without sharing the cost of this pavilion with Gabriel Voisin, who as a leading car and aeroplane manufacturer could better afford it? A model of one of his planes hung on the apartment wall, and the massive urban renewal project displayed alongside bore his name, 'Plan Voisin':

'When the night intervenes the passage of cars along the "autostrada" traces luminous tracks that are like the tails of meteors flashing across the summer heavens.

Two hundred metres above it lie the spacious roof-gardens of these office skyscrapers, planted with spindle-berries, thuyas, laurels and ivy...'

After the poetry, the hook:

'The enormous increase in land values that must result would yield a profit to the state running into millions of francs.'

From the last acts of Goethe's *Faust*, written a century earlier, to Le Corbusier's words, the 'tragedy of development' (in the words of Marshall Berman in *All that is solid melts into air*) would be the major feature of the modern environment.

Saul Steinberg's diploma (Le Corbusier, *Oeuvre complète*)

The artist Willi Baumeister was commissioned to design a pair of stamps to celebrate the Weissenhof exhibition, as well as all the publicity for it. These were not printed.

→

The engraved portrait of Hindenburg, together with the use of Gothic script, marked the beginning of the Nazi Reich: the fearsome features of the former Field Marshall, now president, a reminder of the military power behind Hitler's throne

Le Corbusier had briefly worked alongside Mies van der Rohe in Behrens's Berlin studio, with a grant from the Chaux-de-Fonds art school to study the Arts & Crafts movement. He also met Walter Gropius then. So it was no surprise that he should be asked to participate in the model housing estate proposed for 1927 by the Deutscher Werkbund in Stuttgart, and for which Mies was the master planner.

Originally conceived as economic social housing, it was to become both an ideological battleground and a showcase for individual architects operating at markedly different ends of the housing market. But the resulting similarity – cubic shapes, flat roofs, rendered façades – gave birth to the simplistic title 'International Style', and the coincidental name of Weissenhof Siedlung suggested that this style was white. In fact, there was some colour, not all as strident as on Bruno Taut's 'proletarian house' (his own words). This reflected its red façade onto Mies van der Rohe's sober apartment block, which crowned the estate.

Le Corbusier's retrospectively famous Esprit Nouveau pavilion had been allotted a site at the back of the 1925 Paris Exposition des Arts Décoratifs, hidden at the time of the opening behind a hoarding, to conceal its unfinished state. This time, he was quick to take the key corner site, and his plan for two contrasting house types, vertical and horizontal, exploited the location fully. At the opposite end of the site was a terraced block of flats by Behrens; so, adding the house by Gropius, the old firm was well represented. The idea of a test lot for new ideas on housing had been suggested first by Bruno Taut, following the

formation in 1918 of the socialist 'Arbeitsrat für Kunst' in Berlin:

'Art and People must be one. Art must no longer constitute an enjoyment for a few, but happiness and life for the masses. Unity of the arts, beneath the sheltering wings of the great art of building, is the objective. Henceforth, the artist alone, as the one who gives form to the people's sensibility, is responsible for the visible garb of the new state. He must determine the design, from the city to the coin and the postage stamp.'

Taut's words were supported by the other contemporary radical formation: the 'Novembergruppe', named after the 1918 revolution that overthrew the Kaiser. The group included Mies van der Rohe and Hugo Häring: two contrasting approaches that indicated its stylistic pluralism. Local reaction to the project was more mixed than at Pessac. The communists thought the money should have been spent on simple workers housing, while the leading Stuttgart architects, Bonatz and Schmitthenner, at the other end of the political spectrum, reacted to their exclusion by publishing abusive articles in the local press. This campaign culminated in the oddly comic photomontage of the Weissenhof as an Arab village, published shortly after the Nazis came to power in 1933. The 'strength through joy' movement would surely have enjoyed the opportunity to sunbathe on the Corbusian roof terraces; and indeed, the three-mile-long holiday hotel they built on the Baltic coast took the linear functional style about as far as it could go.

Pál Meller, the site architect for Oud's meticulously functional little houses which stood behind, and in contrast to, Le Corbusier's open planning, would be murdered by the Nazis. The remarkable Margarete Schütte-Lihotzky, designer of the 'Frankfurt kitchen', at the Weissenhof to oversee Ernst May's prefabricated 'Plattenhaus', after working with him in Moscow, survived her imprisonment by the Nazis in Vienna. Almost all the contributors were removed from office or exiled. A competition was held in 1938 to design the military headquarters that were intended to replace a demolished Weissenhof.

Heimatschutz postcard (c.1941). In the 1960s, after the 'economic miracle' in the German Federal Republic, Turkish and Arab 'Gastarbeiter' would come to inhabit similar peripheral early modern estates, if not those granted historical status

In a suggestion for Madame Ocampo, of Argentina, Le Corbusier put forward the idea of a whole cluster of 'Villa Savoye' types, for what he described as a 'Virgillian dream' setting, just outside Buenos Aires. Site specific? Non, merci

The second volume of the *Oeuvre complète* of Le Corbusier and Pierre Jeanneret opened with photographs of the Villa Savoye. This was to be the last exercise in what the Bolsheviks termed 'the style of the Industrial Bourgeoisie', and the Americans – 'the International Style'. Seen from afar, the Villa Savoye did look as if it had just landed; the white render and taut prismatic surfaces creating an illusion of lightness over a rather crude concrete and block construction. It was not until the Harrison House of Kocher and Frey in 1931, and the Case Study houses of Pierre Koenig and Charles Eames in the 1950s, that truly lightweight, industrial component houses were built, in the airy climate of Los Angeles. Ironically, such dwellings now only survive within security patrolled enclaves ('Sentinel Security – Armed Response').

One of the last projects of 1929 contained a clue to the subsequent development – the Maisons Loucheur. This was a project for metal framed and clad component houses, partly supported by and separated from each other by a wall of local masonry: vernacular and industrial, heavy and light material juxtaposed. This theme was also explored in some of the furniture shown at the Salon d'Automne in 1929. To the combination of gleaming metal with shaggy cowhide or pony skin, was added, in the case of the chaise longue, a definite erotic undertow.

In 1929, just a year after the founding meeting of CIAM – the Congrès Internationaux d'Architecture Moderne – for which Le Corbusier had been one of the prime movers, held at the château of Hélène de Mandrot in La Sarraz, Switzerland, he designed a house for her, of primarily loadbearing walls in local stonework and timber. This and other house projects of the period, which reached an apotheosis in the 1935 weekend house, with its unique fusion of vernacular, classical and technological elements, suggested the deliberate opening-up of a distance between himself and the 'International Stylists'.

The incorporation of the primitive into western art, most famously with Picasso's *Demoiselles d'Avignon* of 1907, was perhaps less a matter of naked exploitation than in the case of the colonial resources that helped to shore up the depressed economies of Europe. The huge Colonial Exhibition held in 1931, just outside Paris, attracted six million visitors. Regionalism was on the agenda, seemingly taking on board some of the criticism that had been made by the 'blood and earth' supporters of the Nazis at the time of the Weissenhof Siedlung at Stuttgart.

The Mandrot house however, with its precarious entrance, proved a technical failure. Junctions between the factory-made windows and local in situ masonry didn't work out, and the walls themselves soaked up the water. The little weekend house of 1935, for a Monsieur Félix, built shadily in the name of the company he directed, was more successful. It remains a perfect example of a sophisticated primitivism, the refuge from the demands of industry and the metropolis that provided the wealth for it: a story as old at least as the industrial revolution. And didn't Marie Antoinette play peasants and shepherdesses in the gardens of Versailles, before the real folk arrived?

If the salon furniture within the free plan of the church pavilion seemed to encapsulate the jazz age and the sensuous rhythms of Duke Ellington, the Mandrot house and postwar vernacular derivations suggested a parallel with a similar movement in the music: Charles Mingus's 'Blues and Roots', with the Jazz Workshop collective. Smoothness was left to the cooler West Coast boys, matching the architecture of the Case Study houses.

While Le Corbusier was working on the two Weissenhof houses, a talented Parisian designer, originally from Ireland, was working on a little vacation house project on the Côte d'Azur. She was Eileen Gray, and the house, called E.1027, was for Jean Badovici, the publisher of *L'Architecture Vivante*, and working at that time (1927) on the issue of the magazine that featured the Weissenhof. The house was not occupied until 1929, but, when published in *L'Architecture Vivante*, created quite a stir. For here was an exciting synthesis of the new architecture and décor. Eileen Gray had designed all the furniture and fabrics, as well as weaving the rugs herself. The house was shared until her own, at Castellar, was finished in 1934. The subtly articulated plan was a careful blend of openness and enclosure, in which interior and exterior carry equal weight; a comfortable, even sensuous, alternative to the Corbusian interiors of that time. The site was at Roquebrune, overlooking Cap-Martin, one of Le Corbusier's favourite bathing spots.

Back in Paris, he lost no time in recruiting the brilliant young designer Charlotte Perriand, and the furniture exhibited at the Salon d'Automne in 1929, the product of that collaboration (credited to Le Corbusier), rectified this previous gap in his oeuvre.

This was a purple patch in his career. The airship construction fund stamp by Dubasov – 'from the reindeer of the tundra to the camel of the steppes' – is a reminder of his travels then: the second visit to Moscow, to witness the start on site of the Centrosoyuz project; and there again in 1930, following the trip to South America, to present his city plan for Moscow; designs for the Salvation Army hostel in Paris; the Maison Clarté apartments in Geneva; the Pavillon Suisse in Paris; and his apartment at 24 rue Nungesser-et-Coli, following his marriage to Yvonne Gallis and adoption of French nationality; to be followed by another trip to Algeria.

1930 was the centennial of the French conquest of Algeria and Le Corbusier had been invited to lecture there as part of the colonial celebrations in 1931. He took the opportunity to present his first version of the Obus plan, where more sinuous forms made their appearance, following the outline and contours of the bay. He also took time out to pursue his own version of what would become known as sexual tourism, another aspect of the colonial heritage. That such a sweeping plan could only be realized by a centralized state power was a fact that did not escape the notice of his critics on the left.

Obus plan for Algeria, 1930. (From: Le Corbusier, *Oeuvre complète 1929–34*)

Maison Citrohan (1922–7): a project for the Côte d'Azur. (From: Le Corbusier, *Oeuvre complète 1910–29*)

1939. With Hitler's surcharged 'culture fund' stamps making their appearance – a 'culture' of vast neoclassicism in the cities, 'völkisch' suburbs, colonial expansion and extermination – and the lights about to go out all over Europe, Le Corbusier was to be found in the nude, painting on the walls of the empty villa of Eileen Gray and Jean Badovici, on the Côte d'Azur. Or, in the case of the largest work, under the 'pilotis', measuring two by four metres, 'graffiti' would be more accurate, and it was the term used in the *Oeuvre complète*. Scratched into the concrete surface, before being filled in with black paint, it shows two superimposed figures watched by a third, hand between thighs, with what looks like a swastika dividing breasts. Bullet holes appeared on this wall during the war, as if resistance workers had been shot against it.

In 1940, with the Nazi occupation of Paris, Le Corbusier escaped to Ozon, while Jeanneret and Perriand joined the resistance. Making his peace with the Vichy regime allowed him to continue work, including further versions of the Algiers plan, now with a monumental skyscraper. Like the murals, this work was unsolicited; his links with the Soviet Union were held against him, and with the reprinting in an Algiers newspaper of Alexandre von Senger's poisonous article of 1928, which accused him – and modern architecture – of being the 'Trojan Horse of Bolshevism', he was quickly dropped. His only commissioned design was for a munitions factory, and it appeared in the wartime *Oeuvre complète* as 'L'Usine-vert'. Green, indeed.

The first volume of the *Oeuvre complète* had already contained a sketch for a version of the Maison Citrohan, the front 'pilotis' standing in the water of the Côte d'Azur. After the war, Le Corbusier built a little cabin overlooking the site, and drew up a speculative plan for a holiday village there: the 'Roq et Rob' shell-vaulted, tightly knit housing units stepping down the steep hillside. On 27 August 1963, he died while swimming there, and the little pathway to the beach is now a Corbu heritage trail.

Graffiti at Cap-Martin. (From: Le Corbusier, *Oeuvre complète 1938-46*)

The postwar euphoria was short-lived for the Americans. It wasn't enough that their economy had left the Depression far behind, thanks to a war they had helped to win. Institutionalized paranoia took hold, exemplified by the House of Un-American Activities Committee. 'I call on the Department of Justice to stop this man Einstein', said leading committee member Rankin. 'He is trying to further the spread of communism throughout the world. It's about time the American people got wise to Einstein.'

The Modulor man features on this 1987 stamp and first day cover, marking the Le Corbusier centenary

After 1941 Le Corbusier continued to press his suit with another version of the Algiers plan, this time capped with a giant skyscraper. The highly articulated profile and 'brise soleil' were further indications of the distance now opened up from the earlier flush glazing that had caused problems in both Moscow and Paris. Nevertheless, the plan remained a symbol of colonial domination, but not one that found favour with the regime. He returned to France and made his retreat to the Pyrenees.

Walter Benjamin, who had tried to escape via a similar route, when the Nazis took Paris, was not as fortunate. Held on the Franco-Spanish frontier, and hearing that he was likely to be handed over to the Gestapo, he took his own life.

For Le Corbusier it was a time of painting and writing, including work on the Modulor system of proportional measurement. While lecturing in Princeton, New Jersey, immediately after the war, Le Corbusier arranged a meeting with Albert Einstein, to present his patented Modulor system. This famous photo opportunity of 1946 – apart from giving the lie to Orson Welles's contemporary observation (in Graham Greene's screenplay for *The third man*) that five hundred years of peace and democracy in Switzerland had produced nothing more significant than the cuckoo clock – subsequently elicited the comment from Einstein that it was a language of proportions that 'made the bad difficult and the good easy'.

Nominated to the board of Design Consultants for the proposed headquarters of the United Nations in New York, Le Corbusier, never one to be backward in coming forward, submitted project 23A. The fact that Wallace K. Harrison's winning project bore a striking resemblance to his proposal should have been taken as a compliment, but led to the charge of plagiarism. After the real fiasco of the League of Nations competition in 1927, when his project was robbed of the prize by an absurd technicality, and the farcical Palace of Soviets competition result, when a banal American project was premiated ahead of Le Corbusier's, this disappointment was more of an anticlimax.

Better was to come when Josip Lluís Sert, the Catalan architect who had worked in the atelier at the rue de Sèvres in 1928–30, now Dean of the Graduate School at Harvard, gave him the commission for the Carpenter Center. The basic 'parti' for this Center for the Visual Arts, with its dramatic diagonal ramp forming a processional way through the heart of the building, seemed to refer back to Konstantin Melnikov's pavilion at the 1925 Paris Exposition des Arts Décoratifs: but the architectural vocabulary was totally Corbusian. Of all his concrete buildings, this was the most perfectly realized. Boat builders had to be called in to help construct the curved framework. Yet he declined to attend the opening, and, indeed, never saw the finished project. Now in his seventies, his enthusiasm was elsewhere. Chains had to be installed across the ramps to prevent the wild ones riding motorbikes up and over.

Friedrich Nietzsche, the philosopher who, after Marx, had done so much to explore the contradictions that became the touchstone of the modern world, wrote of two types of new man: the priest and the artist. Le Corbusier was a unique combination of both.

In the 1930s, Le Corbusier's major clients had been the Salvation Army and the revolutionary new Soviet Union; in the 1950s, they were the Dominican monks and the new Indian Republic led by Jawaharlal Nehru. After all his earlier appeals to 'those in authority' had fallen on deaf ears, a visit from two Indians, P.L. Varma and P.N. Thapar, must have seemed manna from heaven: they came to seek his collaboration in the design of the new city of Chandigarh, now the capital of what was left of the state of Punjab after partition from Pakistan. Yet, daunted by the prospect of moving to India, and the low fees, his initial response was to refuse. But when they upped the ante to include exclusive design of the Capitol buildings, and a contract for just two month-long visits each year, he agreed; and with his first site visit in 1951, he seemed to have found a spiritual home, and one that was in contrast to the big-business philistinism of the USA. During this visit he was also invited to design a museum and a private house for the mayor of Ahmedabad, as well as a house for the secretary of the Mill-owners' Association there, which became the Villa Shodhan. The latter led to a further project, a clubhouse for the Association, overlooking the Sabarmati river.

This little palace, a summation of all the Corbusian concepts, was completed in 1954: his first Indian masterpiece. As well as the curved forms within the prismatic envelope, the circular columns within the Citrohan-like solid cross walls, and the roof garden, the favourite ramp first seen in the Villa Savoye is here taken outside to form part of an honorific, triple-height entrance to the 'piano nobile'. This modernist interpretation of the Palladian villa type also shares the idea of distinctive front and garden elevations commanding the landscape, as with similar land-owning clients in Renaissance Italy, but here with a religion that had far greater respect for all forms of life and a philanthropy that mitigated the rigid social hierarchy.

The successful completion of this project and, in 1955, of the chapel at Ronchamp, together with the presentation of the Royal Institute of British Architects' Gold Medal (1953) marked the beginning of an extraordinarily creative decade. But why did that medal have to be inscribed with his old name, and not 'Le Corbusier'? He was miffed.

RONCHAMP (Haute-Saône)

Intérieur de la Chapelle Notre-Dame-du-Haut
Le Corbusier Architecte

The Ronchamp chapel was celebrated in 1965 by this first day cover

Maisons Jaoul,
Neuilly-sur-Seine.
Photographed in 1977

The Sarabhai double house, for Mrs Sarabhai and her son, was in many ways the opposite of the Shodhan house. Yet both derived from earlier prototypes: in this case the shell-vaulted Maison Monol, illustrated in *Vers une architecture*, and the week-end house of 1935. Taken together with the garages and servants' quarters, the result on plan was similar to the holiday housing scheme for Roq et Rob, next to the Eileen Gray villa. This group form became a starting point for what would be known as structuralism, championed by the Dutch architects Aldo van Eyck and Herman Hertzberger. The site may have lent itself to the simpler ground-hugging form, but the result was, and still is, far more successful than the architectonics of Shodhan. The rugged æsthetic of fair-face brick and concrete was also more appropriate in the setting of the Sarabhai's artificial jungle enclave than in the concurrent case of the Jaoul houses in a posh suburb of Paris. Mrs Sarabhai did not want the vaults expressed externally, as they were on the Jaoul houses, and this makes the overall form even more reticent, marred only by the clumsy entrance canopy. The thick grassed roof would also prove a useful climate moderator. Within the structural frame, Le Corbusier placed free-standing elements such as the library, a modernist version of the celebrated study of St Jerome as painted by Antonello da Messina; an extraordinary luxury, seen in the light of the ascetism of the Indian holy men. The Sarabhais, and the other mill-owning families, were however more representative of the new India, combining modernization, necessary to compete in world markets, with a respect for tradition. They had played a significant part in the liberation from British rule, together with Gandhi, whose ashram was in Ahmedabad.

King George VI was the last British monarch to appear on India's stamps. These even went as far as celebrating the 'quit India' movement, compromised for many by its support for the Japanese in the Second World War

With the cave-like vaulted spaces of the Sarabhai double house set in the exotically cultivated landscape of the family estate in the suburbs of Ahmedabad, Le Corbusier had arrived at a version of the Virgilian dream that was the inverse of the sophisticated Miesian glass box built by Philip Johnson at New Canaan in 1949, or the Farnsworth house (1946–9) by Mies van der Rohe himself. That highly refined steel-frame version of Le Corbusier's 'Dom-Ino' skeleton was surely also the ultimate expression of the free façade – another of the 'five points of a new architecture'. And what could be freer than rendering the façades completely transparent?

Another inversion in the Sarabhai house was the favourite honorific ramp, here transformed into a water chute, from the roof down to the garden pool; apparently derived from Anand Sarabhai's favourite story by André Maurois, *Fatapoufs and Thinifers*. What had started out as the shallow concrete shell vaults of the prefabricated Monol housing project of the 1920s had become progressively more substantial. The industrial connotation of the expressed vaults led to the concrete fasçia beam, which contributed to this heavier, but more simple and unified elevation.

The glass box or the concrete cave: two modernist archetypes. High tech or low tech? And with his purchase of the Farnsworth house, adding to his Jaoul house, Lord Palumbo has one of each.

As the Sarabhai house neared completion, the Museum of Modern Art in New York premiered the first film of a new cinematic talent from West Bengal. The film was *Pather Panchali*, a saga of village life based on Bibhuti Banerji's novel, which the director Satyajit Ray had illustrated in 1947. Shot on fragments of film stock, using his own money, it was finally taken over by the new government in return for the producer's rights. As well as Ray, the film also introduced the master musician Ravi Shankar to Western audiences – through its melo-drama, in the original Greek sense of the word.

From then on, it was not just Le Corbusier who was entranced by the culture of post-colonial India. The New York jazz musicians, some of whom had taken Muslim names, were the first to see the extended harmonic possibilities of Ravi Shankar's music, not to mention its expressive impact: John Coltrane in particular. The 1961 sessions that produced the bril-liant 'Spiritual' with Eric Dolphy also saw the explicit reference: 'India'. It was recorded in November 1961, as the last major building in Chandigarh was being completed: the Palace of Assembly.

The conquest of Everest in 1953, just in time for the coronation of Queen Elizabeth II of England, was commemorated by India with both 2 and 14 anna values

One of the highlights of 1959 was an exhibition of Le Corbusier's architecture, painting, sculpture and tapestries, at the Building Centre in London. As well as stunningly evocative photographs of such recent projects as Ronchamp and the Mill-owners' building in Ahmedabad, there were superb hardwood models of the Chandigarh plan and of individual buildings there, constructed by master carpenters Rattan Singh and Dani Ram. The sheer scale and power of the newly completed buildings was in dramatic contrast to the slick curtain walling that had become the norm in the West. Le Corbusier was quick to point out how this monumentality had been achieved at a fraction of the cost of the United Nations building in New York. In fact his exclusion from this project seems, in retrospect, one of the best things that could have happened for him, as his talent flowered more completely under ideologies quite opposite to that one. Le Corbusier, after all his earlier appeals to industry and mass production, retained a metaphysical side to his character, in which the ancient art of numerology played a major part.

'On 28 March, 1951, at Chandigarh, at sunset, we had set off in a jeep across the still empty site of the capital — Varma, Fry, Pierre Jeanneret and myself. Never had the spring been so lovely, the air so pure after a storm on the day before, the horizons so clear, the mango trees so gigantic and magnificent. We were at the end of our task (the first): we had created the city (the town plan).

I noticed then that I had lost the box of the Modulor, of the only Modulor strip in existence, made by Soltan in 1945, which had not left my pocket for six years…a grubby box, splitting at the edges. During that last visit of the site before my return to Paris, the Modulor had fallen from the jeep on to the soil of the fields that were to disappear to make way for the capital. It is there now, in the very heart of the place, integrated in the soil. Soon it will flower in all the measurements of the first city of the world to be organized all of a piece in accordance with that harmonious scale.'

(Le Corbusier, 'Album du voyage', India 1951.)

The clean slate.
(From: Le Corbusier, *Modulor 2*)

The doorway to democracy: the giant door to the Assembly building at Chandigarh was constructed from modular panels hand-painted by Le Corbusier. The smooth glaze and bright colours, while in dramatic contrast to the rough concrete, lack the civic gravitas of their embossed equivalents found in the first ideal cities of the Renaissance

The granting of independence to India in 1947 by the Attlee government was another great moment for democracy, in spite of the bloodshed that accompanied the brutal partition. What Lenin and the Bolsheviks had achieved with a minority coup in 1917 was won in India by more open methods, including a tactic that would have lasting results elsewhere: Gandhi's method of massive non-violent resistance. Yet the concept had its roots in America, a hundred years earlier, with Thoreau's *On the duty of civil disobedience*, written after the first year of living in his self-built hut by Walden Pond. Thoreau wrote the essay after being imprisoned for failing to pay his poll tax. No Virgilian dream without the dollar. With the adoption of Gandhi's tactics by Martin Luther King and the NAACP for the civil rights movement in the USA, the concept came full circle.

With Gandhi's assassination in 1948, it was left to Nehru to continue forward during the Cold War, with the five principles of 'panch shila': non-interference in the internal affairs of other states, mutual respect for territorial integrity and sovereignty, mutual non-aggression, mutual aid, peaceful co-existence. These were announced in 1954 after a meeting with Zhou Enlai, and were taken up by the Bandung Conference in the following year, as Le Corbusier and the team completed the plan for Chandigarh.

Le Corbusier had at last found someone in authority who would support him. But with Nehru's death in 1964, and his own in 1965, the plan would never be fully realized. Nehru had already vetoed the governor's palace, as inappropriate for the new socialist democracy. So Le Corbusier's master plan lost its crowning element, together with the sunken garden intended to help mediate between the different scales of open space: the vastness in deliberate contrast to the congestion of existing cities such as Calcutta or Bombay. This landscaping, derived from a conflation of Mughal 'charbagh' or paradise garden with his own earlier 'ville radieuse', was an essential part of the grand design that has been neglected. Le Corbusier's love of hierarchy found its clearest expression in the Chandigarh plan: the hand-built modern city. But within the hierarchical plan there was still no room for the building labourers, who remain in the peripheral shanty towns.

Yet Chandigarh was a unique attempt at a synthesis of the monumental with the democratic; and India offered a more sustainable future than either the globalization of American consumer capitalism or the Stalinism of the USSR and China. If the First World War and the Russian revolution had marked the end of the old regimes of that era, mass non-violent resistance would lead to future democratization after an era of increasing state power.

The business of Architecture is to establish emotional relationships
by means of raw materials.
Architecture goes beyond utilitarian needs.
Architecture is a plastic thing.
The spirit of order, a unity of intention.
The sense of relationships; architecture deals with quantities.
Passion can create drama out of inert stone.

Le Corbusier:
Vers une architecture, 1923

Bibliography

These are the principal books used in writing this text, grouped by section. Place of publication is London, unless otherwise given.

Brown, Theodore M, *The work of G. Rietveld architect*, Utrecht: Bruna, 1958

Derwig, Jan, & Erik Mattie, *Functionalism in the Netherlands*, Amsterdam: Architectura & Natura, 1995

Friedman, Mildred (ed.), *De Stijl 1917–1931: visions of utopia*, Oxford: Phaidon, 1982

Fuchs, R.H, *Dutch painting*, Thames & Hudson, 1978

Groenendijk, Paul, & Piet Vollard, *Guide to modern architecture in the Netherlands*, Rotterdam: 010 Publishers, 1987

Jelles, E.J, & C.A. Alberts, *Duiker 1890–1935*, Amsterdam: Forum, 1972

Lemoine, Serge, *Mondrian and De Stijl*, Art Data, 1987

Molema, Jan, *The new movement in the Netherlands 1924–1936*, Rotterdam: 010 Publishers, 1996

Overy, Paul, *De Stijl*, Thames & Hudson, 1991

Overy, Paul, & others, *The Rietveld Schröder house*, Butterworth Architecture, 1988

Mart Stam: documentation of his work 1920–1965, RIBA, 1970

Schama, Simon, *The embarrassment of riches*, Collins, 1987

Baer, Nancy Van Norman, *Theatre in revolution*, Thames & Hudson, 1991

Cohen, Jean-Louis, *Le Corbusier and the mystique of the USSR*, Princeton: Princeton University Press, 1992

Cohen, Jean-Louis, *Scenes of the world to come*, Paris: Flammarion, 1995

Ginzburg, Moisei, *Style and epoch* [1924], Cambridge Mass: MIT Press, 1982

Gozak, Andrei, & Andrei Leonidov, *Ivan Leonidov*, New York: Rizzoli, 1988

Gray, Camilla, *The great experiment: Russian art 1863–1922*, Thames & Hudson, 1962

Khan-Magomedov, Selim O, *Alexandr Vesnin and Russian constructivism*, Lund Humphries, 1986

Khan-Magomedov, Selim O, *Pioneers of Soviet architecture*, Thames & Hudson, 1987

Kopp, Anatole, *Constructivist architecture in the USSR*, Academy Editions, 1985

Kopp, Anatole, *Town and revolution: Soviet architecture and city planning 1917–1935*, Thames & Hudson, 1969

Lissitzky, El, *Russia: an architecture for world revolution* [1930], Lund Humphries, 1970

Marshall, Herbert (ed.), *Mayakovsky*, Dobson, 1965

Milner, John, *Russian revolutionary art*, Oresko Books, 1979

Morosow, Sergei, *Sowjetische Fotografen: 1917–1940*, Berlin: Elefanten Press, 1980

Nettl, J.P, *The Soviet achievement*, Thames & Hudson, 1967

Sarabianev, Dmitri V, & Natalia L. Adaskina, *Popova*, Thames & Hudson, 1990

Shvidkovsky, O.A, *Building in the USSR: 1917–32*, Studio Vista, 1971

Woroszylski, Wiktor, *The life of Mayakovsky*, Gollancz, 1972

Zhadova, Larissa (ed.), *Tatlin*, Thames & Hudson, 1988

Le Corbusier, *Towards a new architecture* [1923], Rodker, 1927

Le Corbusier, *Oeuvre complète*, Zurich: Girsberger, 1910– (8 volumes)

Le Corbusier, *Modulor 2*, Faber & Faber, 1958

Besset, Maurice, *Who was Le Corbusier?* Geneva: Skira, 1968

Boudon, Philippe, *Lived-in architecture*, Lund Humphries, 1972

Colomina, Beatriz, 'Battle lines: E.1027', in: Agrest, Diana, & others (ed.), *The sex of architecture*, New York: Abrams, 1996

Curtis, William, *Le Corbusier: ideas and forms*, Oxford: Phaidon, 1986

Frampton, Kenneth, & Yukio Futagawa (ed.), 'Le Corbusier: Mill-owners' Association building and Carpenter Center for Visual Arts', *Global Architecture*, no.37, 1975

Jenger, Jean, *Le Corbusier: architect of a new age*, Thames & Hudson, 1996

Kirsch, Karin, *The Weissenhof Siedlung*, New York: Rizzoli, 1989

Krustrup, Mogens, *Porte émail*, Copenhagen: Arkitektens Forlag, 1991

Raeburn, Michael, & Victoria Wilson (ed.), *Le Corbusier: architect of the century*, Arts Council, 1987

Dunster, David, *Key buildings of the twentieth century, volume 1: houses 1900–1944*, Architectural Press, 1985

The Dutch PTT, Design Museum, 1990

Glanville, Brian, *Soccer nemesis*, Secker & Warburg, 1955

New, Anthony S.B, *The observer's book of postage stamps*, Warne, 1967

Pidgeon, Monica, & Robin Middleton (ed.), 'Heroic relics', *Architectural Design*, December 1967

Rendall, Ivan, *Reaching for the skies*, BBC Books, 1988

Roth, Alfred (ed.), *The new architecture*, Zurich: Les Éditions d'Architecture, 1940

Smithson, Alison, & Peter Smithson, with Christopher Woodward (ed.), 'The heroic period of modern architecture', *Architectural Design*, December 1965

Speciale catalogus, The Hague: Nederlandsche Vereeniging van Postzegelhandelaren, 52nd edition, 1993

Timms, Edward, & Peter Collier (ed.), *Visions and blueprints*, Manchester: Manchester University Press, 1988

Wohl, Robert, *A passion for wings*, Yale University Press, 1994